LAND
OF LOST
MONSTERS

Man Against Beast:
The Prehistoric Battle for the Planet

LAND OF LOST MONSTERS

Man Against Beast: The Prehistoric Battle for the Planet

Ted Oakes
with Amanda Kear, Annie Bates and
Kathryn Holmes

The author would like to pay special thanks to Amanda Kear, Annie Bates and Kathryn Holmes for their work on the book.

Hydra Publishing
50 Mallard Rise
Irvington, New York 10533

This book is published to accompany the television series *Land of Lost Monsters*, first broadcast on Animal Planet in 2003.
Series producer: Andy Byatt
Executive producer: Mike Gunton
Producer: Andrew Graham-Brown

First published in 2003 by BBC Worldwide Ltd.
Copyright © Ted Oakes 2003.
The moral right of the author has been asserted.

ISBN 1 59258 005 X

First American Edition published in 2003
02 03 04 05 10 9 8 7 6 5 4 3 2 1

Published in the United States by Hydra Publishing,
50 Mallard Rise, Irvington, New York 10533

A catalog record for this book is available from the Library of Congress

Commissioning editors: Nicky Copeland and
Shirley Patton
Project editor: Sarah Lavelle
Copy editor: Ben Morgan
Art director: Linda Blakemore
Designer: Martin Hendry
Production controller: Kenneth McKay
Picture researchers: Deirdre O'Day and Miriam Hyman
Maps and figures by Map Creation Ltd
Illustrations on pages 56 and 58 by Peter Murray

Set in Garamond 3 and Univers Extended
Printed and bound in France by Imprimerie Pollina,
s.a. L89217
Color separations by Radstock Reproductions,
Midsomer Norton

Distributed by St. Martin's Press

Picture credits
BBC Worldwide would like to thank the following individuals and organisations for providing photographs and for permission to reproduce copyright material. While every effort has been made to trace and acknowledge copyright holders, we would like to apologise should there be any errors or omissions.
a = above; b = below; l = left; r = right

Ardea London: Hans & Judy Beste, Australia 47; John Daniels 5(iii), 84; Ferrero-Labat 24; Jean-Paul Ferrero 41, 44–5, 75; Kenneth W. Fink 186; Martin W. Grosnick 116; Chris Harvey 5(i), 14; Arthur Hayward 119; M. Watson 179; Andrey Zvoznikov 84. Australian National University, Canberra: 54. Annie Bates: 163, 165, 194r, 197. Bishop Museum, Honolulu: B. Patnoi 168. Glenn Carwithen 57, 67, 80. Bruce Coleman Collection: Alain Compost 5(v), 158; Werner Layer 77b; Hans Reinhard 5(iv), 120. Bruce Coleman Inc., New York: 2; E. & P. Bauer 184; Jeff Foott 157; Rinie van Meurs 155; Hans Reinhard 190a. Corbis: 5(ii), 42, 144–5, 160–1, 199. Department of Palaeontology and Palaeo-environmental Studies, Transvaal Museum, Pretoria: 27r. George Chaloupka Collection: 71. Getty Images/National Geographic 131. Andrew Graham-Brown: 38, 129, 134, 192, 194. Kevin Hastings: 136, 139. Images of Africa Photobank: David Keith Jones 16. Frederick Kruger (1831–99), albumen silver photograph *c*. 1877, gift of Mrs Beryl M. Curl/National Gallery of Victoria, Melbourne: 64. Lithic Casting Lab, Illinois: Peter Bostrum 132–3; Dr Adrian Hannus 154. Brian McDairmant: 61, 63, 80. Mary Evans Picture Library: 173. Nature Picture Library: 72, 171, 176, 178; Michael Pitts 166. National Geographic Image Collection (October 1967, pp. 488–9): 181. Natural History Museum, London: 27l, 29, 73, 91, 101, 109. NHPA: Nigel Dennis 6; Daniel Henchin 94; Jonathan & Angela Scott 23. Novosti Photo Library: 102. Ted Oakes: 11, 69, 78, 82. Oxford Scientific Films: 117; Henry Ausloos 110; Clive Bromhall 28; Michael Brooke 175; Mark Jones 150. Robert Harding Picture Library: 77a, 98; Eberhard Brunner 156; F. Jalain 97. Science Photo Library: 36, 49, 114–15, 124–5, 190b; John Reader 19b. Warwick Sloss 1. Te Papa Museum, Wellington: 187, 188. Dr Hartmut Thieme, Institut für Denkmalpflege, Hanover: 35. Associate Professor Rod Wells, Flinders University, Adelaide: 59.

CONTENTS

INTRODUCTION

Prehistory is one subject we are taught little about at school. While we devote months committing to memory the exploits of European explorers and pioneers, we learn nothing about how humans first journeyed beyond Africa to discover Earth's continents and animals. This is despite the fact that these events are among the most epic in history, the moments when people first set foot in Australia, the Americas, Eurasia, Madagascar, New Zealand and the Pacific islands and came face to face with creatures that would stretch the imaginations of Hollywood scriptwriters. However, unlike the science-fiction fantasies depicted in films like *Jurassic Park* and *One Million Years BC*, the monsters discussed here were real. This may be the first book ever written that provides a global overview of our journey beyond Africa and the *Monsters We Met*.

There have been three great eras in the history of animal life. The first was the Palaeozoic, a time of armoured fish and colossal insects. The second was the Mesozoic, famously the 'age of the dinosaurs', which ended 65 million years ago when an asteroid 10 km (6 miles) across crashed into the sea off Mexico with an explosive force greater than that of the world's Cold War nuclear arsenals. From the ashes of this catastrophe emerged the era in which we now live, the Cenozoic. This third era has been dominated by the survivors – mammals, birds, crocodiles and turtles. Freed from competition with the dinosaurs, these animals

◄ Humans met monsters as we explored Earth. Some, like Africa's white rhinoceros, evolved together with us and survive today. Others beyond Africa are now extinct.

evolved to fill their ecological roles and new lumbering giants were born. It was these new 'megafauna' that humans met millions of years later as we took our first tentative steps beyond Africa.

The term 'megafauna' simply means 'large animals'. For some as yet undiscovered natural law, the majority of animals today, like elephants, horses and ostriches, are usually larger than 44 kg (97 lb), or less than a few kilograms like mice, squirrels and hedgehogs, but there are relatively few in between. The Cenozoic, 'the age of the mammals', is divided by geologists into six epochs spanning the last 65 million years. For the purposes of our story, we are mostly interested in the last of those epochs, the Pleistocene, the time from about 1.8 million years ago to the present day. Many researchers recognize a seventh epoch at the end of the Pleistocene called the Holocene, marking the end of the last period of glaciation 10,000 years ago. In many ways the Holocene can be seen to be just an extension of the Pleistocene, a time when modern humans met monsters.

The word 'monster' is used in this book to refer to the megafauna, still living or now extinct, that the first human explorers discovered; certainly some Pleistocene creatures like 'Ice-age' mammoths and sabre-tooth cats appear monstrous to us now. But for every extinct large animal that we know about, there are many others that would inspire equal awe, were it not for the fact that evidence for them lies buried in dusty labs and obscure academic journals. It is not only extinct giants that can spark our imagination for reconstructing the past – there are living monsters too. Today we take for granted the existence of the few surviving megafauna like camels, tigers and Komodo dragons, but if we encountered them without prior knowledge, we might think of them as monsters too.

One of the reasons why few people are aware of these extinct animals and their importance to the human story is the impression that they existed only in some deep and irrelevant past. A surprising truth that will emerge here is just how recent the demise of the megafauna was, and how their legacy continues to affect us today. Some of the monsters discussed in this book, like the mermaid-like Steller's sea cow (*Hydrodamalis gigas*), were alive only a few hundred years ago, while others that we think died out long ago are in fact recent departures. While making the television

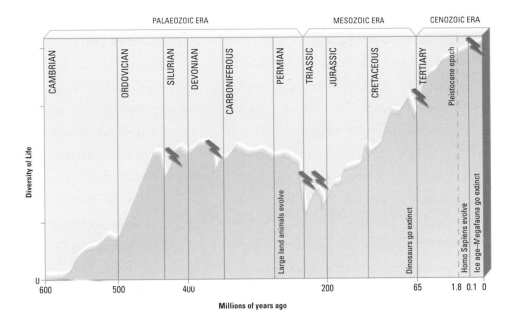

PALAEOZOIC ERA | **MESOZOIC ERA** | **CENOZOIC ERA**

CAMBRIAN · ORDOVICIAN · SILURIAN · DEVONIAN · CARBONIFEROUS · PERMIAN · TRIASSIC · JURASSIC · CRETACEOUS · TERTIARY · Pleistocene epoch

Diversity of Life

Large land animals evolve

Dinosaurs go extinct

Homo Sapiens evolve

Ice age–Megafauna go extinct

600   500   400   200   65   1.8 0.1 0

Millions of years ago

▲ The time scale of life shows that there have been five mass extinctions over the last 600 million years, with a sixth affecting large animals at the end of the Pleistocene.

series, we came across the remains of extinct animals preserved so well that hair was still attached to their bodies. For this story an appreciation of the scale of time is everything. If the years that have passed since the death of the dinosaurs were laid out as a 100-metre sprint, it would be only in the final metre that the mass extinction of the megafauna and our own rise as a new species of mammal occurred. If further proof were needed of just how recent these events are, one only has to look at the fact that no new animal species has arisen since then. There simply hasn't been enough time. In practical terms, that means that all of the animals alive today, from bumblebees to pigeons and mice, also lived alongside less familiar monsters. Envisaging these everyday creatures living alongside extinct giants helps us to re-create the world our ancestors experienced.

Many theories have been proposed to explain the end-Pleistocene mass extinction, including pandemic disease, astronomical events, continental drift, volcanic explosions, climate and even human hunting. One of the peculiar features of this most recent period of extinction is that it seemed to affect mostly large animals. Scientists have debated its causes for decades. They are right to be passionate about this prehistory because any force that can exterminate most of the world's large animals so recently is perhaps a threat to living megafauna like ourselves and is worth investigating. Given this, it is amazing that the money spent annually on researching this phenomenon throughout the world is less than the price of one military aircraft.

Many of the experts who investigate this event specialize in one science (for example, palaeontology, climatology, archaeology) and usually in just one region of the world. One of the goals of this book is to try to make sense of the scientific arguments for the causes of this great extinction by providing for the first time a global portrait of the world of monsters and of their human discoverers.

There is also something satisfying about knowing where you come from. Most people know where their parents and grandparents were born, but few would be able to identify where their more distant relatives lived only a few thousand years ago or what life was like. The recent past was a time of great climatic, ecological and cultural change when we as a species finally became what we would understand to be human: living in social communities, using complex technology, language, art and culture, thinking, laughing and feeling. If you want to understand yourself, then visualizing this past is a great place to start.

Reconstructing prehistory also allows us to question many assumptions about prehistoric people and animals. For example, most people are happy to use the words 'explorers', 'pioneers' or 'discovered' when referring to modern European adventurers like Christopher Columbus, Captain Cook or Magellan, but baulk at using these same terms when discussing the ancestors of today's Native Americans or Australian Aborigines. This is partly because of numerous and inaccurate portrayals of Ice-age humans (and even living indigenous people) in feature films, television documentaries, museums and scientific literature, which depict them as grunting subhumans lacking modern mental or verbal

▲ The ancestors of today's indigenous peoples discovered many regions of Earth thousands of years before Europeans. Their pioneering achievements have been overlooked.

abilities. This is wrong. All humans on Earth have been cognitively modern – that is, they had brains like yours and mine – for at least 100,000 years, and probably much longer. The available evidence shows that whatever creatures our ancestors witnessed, they would have understood them, talked about them and behaved in much the same way that people alive today would.

Another reason why our prehistory has been overlooked is that it leaves, as Jared Diamond of the University of California in Los Angeles has noted, most of the dramatic events to non-Europeans rather than Europeans, who have tended to write history. Aboriginal Australians, natives of the New World, Africans and Polynesians are usually excluded from our popular understanding of how Earth was explored, by the fact that their origins, achievements and existence are rarely mentioned. A good illustration of this is a news story reported in 2002 that claimed that Chinese traders 'discovered' North America 70 years before Columbus, and Australia 350 years before Captain Cook. Amazingly, this and other such reports make no mention of the resident Native American and Aboriginal societies that undeniably pioneered life in those continents many thousands of years before Chinese or European adventurers. It is because of these continuing misrepresentations, together with the legends told by indigenous peoples themselves, that we end up concluding either that these native peoples always lived where they do, or that they arrived in an animal-like state. Attempting to reconstruct the moments when people discovered the continents and their monsters has driven home the view that those original explorers could not have achieved what they did without modern brains, culture and sophisticated and adaptable technologies.

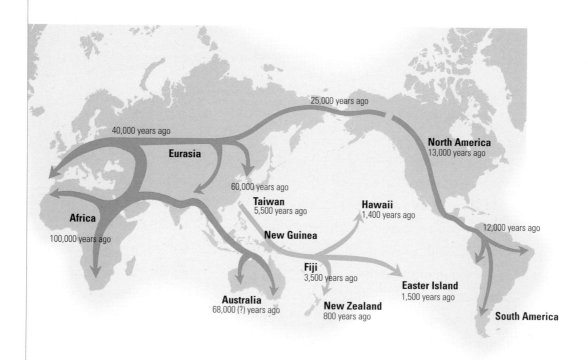

▲ Map showing the probable routes and dates by which modern humans discovered the continents of Earth and the monsters that inhabited them.

While it may seem silly to attempt to dramatize those moments of arrival, it is actually a powerful way of investigating the past. Most of the literature relating to these subjects is inaccessible to ordinary people, either physically, or because it is written by experts from diverse fields who use inaccessible terminology. Fortunately scientists are beginning to gain new insight by sharing their research with those studying other disciplines. This, together with improved dating methods and new techniques like experimental archaeology and palaeoecology, is helping us to unravel the past. Visually reconstructing this new understanding is a great way to frame questions about what really happened to Earth's monsters, which might help us to understand not only ourselves but also the living world of the planet now.

This book is structured as a chronological journey. Chapter 1 explores our recent evolution as a new species of African great ape and how our long relationship with that continent's megafauna changed them and us. Africa is the birthplace of our species and our lengthy occupation there means that its animals have evolved together with us. Could our African history explain everyday phenomena like dangerous African animals, our fear of the dark or our fascination with big cats? Chapter 2 describes the creatures that the ancestors of today's Aborigines encountered when they first arrived in Australia perhaps more than 60,000 years ago. At that time humans were locked out of most of Eurasia by an ice age. The first people to arrive in Australia had to come by boat because that continent had been an island for millions of years. Chapter 3 looks at how the ancestors of Europeans pioneered their Ice-age world 35,000 years ago, in an arctic Wild West with a distinctly African-looking set of monsters. Both Chapters 2 and 3 take a close look at how climate may have influenced the extinction of those continents' megafauna. Chapter 4 investigates the discovery of the New World 13,000 years ago by the ancestors of today's Native Americans, the biggest land-grab by humans since we left Africa. Chapter 5 looks at the more recent island invasions by the Polynesians with a special focus on Madagascar, New Zealand and Hawaii. Finally, the Conclusion tries to make sense of this whirlwind tour of global prehistory and its meaning for us today.

1

AFRICA

● 6 million to 100,000 years ago

Have you ever wondered why Africa has so many large and dangerous animals? Or why we find films about monsters so enthralling? The answers to these questions could lie deep in our past, when our ancestors lived alongside Africa's terrifying megafauna. Do our African origins explain our unique relationship with that continent's animals, their continued survival and even how one species, *Homo sapiens*, came to rule the planet?

◀ Africa's living monsters evolved with humans, which may explain why many survived. Megafauna like African elephants (*Loxodonta africana*) dramatically alter the landscape in which they live.

Mountains of Creation

In order to understand our unique relationship with Africa's animals, we need to know some history. Especially important is the story of a geological event that gave rise to a new group of monsters, and there is a clue to this event in our genes. DNA comparisons reveal that our closest relatives in the animal world are the great apes of Africa, with the two living species of chimpanzee being our nearest relatives, and the gorilla slightly more distant. But what created the differences between us and the other great apes? The answer to that question lies in part in the formation of a dramatic chain of mountains and valleys in East Africa some 6 million years ago.

▲ The formation of Africa's Great Rift Valley may have accelerated the otherwise drying climate, so that one group of great apes was eventually forced to leave the trees and learn to walk.

Family Fortunes

Six million years ago, during the Miocene epoch, the common ancestor of chimpanzees and humans lived in the vast tropical forests that stretched unbroken from the Atlantic coast of Africa to the Indian Ocean. At this time the Great Rift Valley, which now runs from Malawi to Israel, started to form. As the land slipped on each side of a massive fault in the Earth's crust, the western side was pushed upwards into mountain chains, while the east side sank into spectacular valleys. These new mountains, together with an earlier drying of the climate, had a dramatic impact on the plants and animals of the region. While tropical forest remained in the west, the mountains cast a rain shadow over East Africa, helping to create a more arid and open savannah landscape. This separation of Africa into two parts laid the foundations for human history. The great apes were divided; those stuck in the forest to the west of the Rift Valley evolved into modern chimpanzees and gorillas, while those in the arid environment to the east were forced out of the trees and on the road to humanity. Geology changes history. If the Rift Valley had not formed when and where it did, we might still be living in trees. As it is, Earth now crawls with more than 6 billion of our species, *Homo sapiens*, while today we experiment on, exhibit, destroy the homes of, and even eat the other great apes, so that now they number only a few thousand each.

Scientists use the term 'hominid' to refer to those species in our line that evolved after our evolutionary split with chimpanzees. Although chimpanzees have had 6 million years to accrue changes since our paths diverged, most scientists think the early hominids shared some important characteristics with chimps. Fossils provide intriguing clues.

First Steps

The oldest hominid fossils so far discovered may date from 4.5 million years ago and come from East Africa. These few bones suggest that early members of our group, such as *Ardipithecus ramidus*, could walk upright, if awkwardly, and spent at least some time in trees. Their ability to walk upright is inferred from their leg-bone and hip-bone structure, but they must also have lived partly in trees, because their curved hand bones and huge finger muscle attachments indicate a continuing adaptation to life in the trees.

The oldest-known hominid for which we have a good selection of skeletal remains is *Australopithecus* ('southern ape'), which first appeared around 4 million years ago. There were many species of australopithecine, all of which were surprisingly small animals, only 1–1.5 m (3–5 feet) tall.

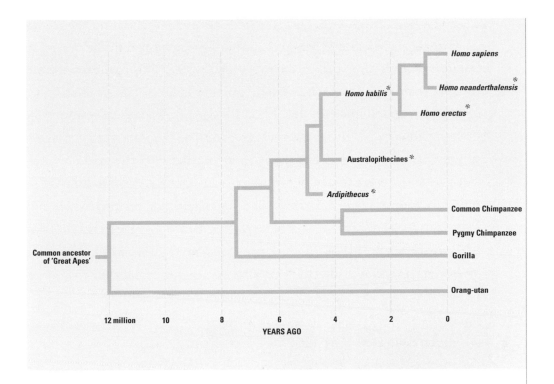

Common ancestor of 'Great Apes'

Ardipithecus *

Australopithecines *

Homo habilis *

Homo sapiens

Homo neanderthalensis *

Homo erectus *

Common Chimpanzee

Pygmy Chimpanzee

Gorilla

Orang-utan

12 million   10   8   6   4   2   0

YEARS AGO

▲ Monster ape family tree. Chimpanzees split from two-legged apes more than 5 million years ago. Extinct groups are shown with an asterisk.

▶ Footprints left by an australopithecine family preserved in volcanic ash at Lactoli, Tanzania – proof that our relatives walked on two legs at least 3.5 million years ago.

The sexes showed a remarkable difference in size and robustness, with the males being much larger than females, and they probably lived in extended family groups, as chimpanzees do today. They may have eaten fruit, plant roots and even abandoned animal carcasses. Their fossils indicate that they lived a very different lifestyle from that of other animals – leg bones showing clear adaptations for walking, though curved fingers and toes suggest that they also spent time in trees. Positive proof of two-legged walking comes from 3.5-million-year-old footprints preserved in volcanic ash at Laetoli, Tanzania. These footprints were left by a small group of *Australopithecus* – perhaps a mother, father and their child.

Were we to meet australopithecines in Africa today, we might well mistake them for a small troop of chimpanzees strangely far from tree

cover, with an unusual ability to walk on two legs. These small hominids pioneered this new and dangerous two-legged lifestyle on Africa's predator-rich savannah. One species of *Australopithecus* was almost certainly the ancestor of our genus, *Homo*.

For 3–4 million years, hominid species lived only in Africa. This is such a vast period of time that it is difficult for us truly to grasp its enormity or understand its implications. Most scientists have overlooked how dangerous this African 'boot camp' was for our ancestors and how this era may have shaped us, our minds and our relationship with Earth's animals. If we want to understand ourselves, the megafauna and our current domination of the planet, then this period in our history is worth considering in some depth.

▲ Our monstrous relative *Australopithecus afarensis* pioneered the dangerous world beyond the trees.

◀ If we found a group of australopithecines today, we might mistake them for chimpanzees. Several species existed at the same time, only one of which gave rise to our genus, *Homo*.

On Deadly Ground

Although the transition from tree-dwelling apes to walking hominids sounds glorious, in reality it must have been a nightmare. As our ancestors were forced down from the trees by the drying climate and began to walk, they must have been vulnerable. African savannahs harbour a bewildering variety of large, well-armed and extremely dangerous animals, which in turn are preyed on by some of the world's more fearsome predators. This and succeeding worlds were not grassy utopias but instead lethal arenas, in Africa's case prowled by pack-hunting carnivores like giant, flesh-shearing hyenas (*Crocuta*, *Hyaena*, *Pachycrocuta*), wolf-sized, blade-toothed dogs (*Canis*, *Cuon*), bizarre forms of big cat

DINOFELIS

Dinofelis is the name given to several sabre-toothed cats that lived in the savannahs of Africa, Europe and Asia between 5 and 1.4 million years ago.

Dinofelis was an ambush predator that had to stalk within close range, taking its prey by surprise. The cat's foreleg structure suggests that it was capable of climbing trees, like modern leopards, so even in their safest hiding places our ancestors were in mortal danger. Several australopithecine skulls have been found with *Dinofelis* tooth marks on them – chilling evidence of our long history as prey.

▲ For most of human history we have been prey for monsters (like *Dinofelis*) rather than predators.

▶ Humans have a long shared history with big cats like African lions (*Panthera leo*), first as prey and then as competitors. Lions' facial expressions suggest they see us as competition.

▲ Most of today's deadly African monsters are vegetarians. Hippopotamus (*Hippopotamus amphibius*) look harmless but actually kill more people than Africa's predators.

(*Megantereon*), and even prides of lions (*Panthera leo*). That, it would seem, is a less than ideal environment to be a metre tall and learning to walk. Patches of trees must have seemed like attractive sanctuaries to our early ancestors, though even these refuges were vulnerable to tree-climbing cats. We could be forgiven for thinking that the predators should have exterminated our line before it began. But monstrous predators were probably only half the problem.

DEINOTHERE

Deinotheres were gigantic cousins of modern elephants that lived from 20 to 1.5 million years ago and were abundant during the time of the australopithecines. Males stood 4 m (13 feet) tall at the shoulder, while females were slightly shorter, at 3.5 m (11½ feet). Like modern elephants, deinotheres were browsers rather than grazers – they fed on trees and shrubs rather than grass. Although they were plant-eaters, like today's elephants their immense size and baby-defending instincts would have made them dangerous. The deinotheres had specially shaped tusks and probably fed by knocking over trees and stripping the bark. Australopithecines needed to keep a wary eye on Africa's plant-eaters.

▼ **Deinotheres evolved together with humans over millions of years.**

Few people realize that Africa's most dangerous large animals are actually its killer vegetarians. Today a tourist visiting an African park is far more likely to be killed or injured by plant-eaters than carnivores. Of the five most dangerous large animals in Africa today, four are herbivores (elephant, African buffalo, hippo and rhino) and only one is a predator (the lion). In a past world without human-caused habitat destruction, it seems likely that large, dangerous animals were even more plentiful.

Given the variety and fierceness of Africa's megafauna, it is remarkable that we survived at all.

Traditional narratives of early hominid life emphasized our ancestors' supposed hunting prowess. When hominid fossils were first recovered in the nineteenth and twentieth centuries, scientists felt they needed to demonstrate how human-like these creatures were – the discovery of animals that were broadly vegetarian and skulked in trees would not have advanced their efforts to convince the world they had discovered our noble ancestors. Palaeoanthropologist Raymond Dart of the University of Witwatersrand in South Africa interpreted australopithecine fossils found in several South African caves as evidence that early hominids were meat-eating cave-dwellers. The numerous animal bones discovered in these same caves he interpreted as the remains of kills, brought home to be eaten in relative safety. Dart even identified what he thought were man-made tools, including the bones and jaws of large antelopes. These were interpreted as hunting clubs, saws and digging tools. Fractures in the hominid fossils were judged to be the result of intergroup warfare with these 'weapons'.

It is only recently that the horrible truth has begun to unfold, thanks to careful re-examination of these fossils by palaeontologist C.K. Brain of the Transvaal Museum, Pretoria. Far from being cave-dwelling hunters, it now seems unlikely that our australopithecine ancestors lived in caves or hunted large animals at all. Instead, a closer examination of the fractured bones now suggests that australopithecines and other large animals were dragged into caves by ape-eating carnivores and bone-gnawing porcupines looking for a quiet place to enjoy their meal. Trees that overhang cave entrances are perfect ambush and larder sites for cats such as leopards. Their leftovers (in this case our ancestors' bones) would have fallen into the caves beneath and so become preserved for future scientists to misinterpret.

Brain's theory is supported by a gruesome piece of evidence from one of these South African caves, the Swartkrans excavation site. Here a young australopithecine skull was found, bearing two holes exactly matching the lower canines of a big cat. Perhaps they were made during

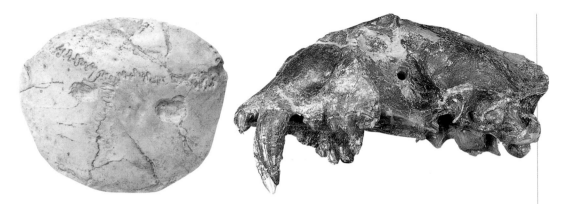

▲ An *Australopithecus robustus* skull (left) found in the Transvaal, South Africa. It features two puncture marks that match the fangs of ape-hunting big cats like *Dinofelis* (skull, right).

the kill or as the cat dragged its victim up a tree. Today carnivore lairs in South African caves have turned up fossils of 140 australopithecines, many bearing tooth and claw marks from big cats and hyenas. The high proportion of primate fossils in these caves suggests that at least one species of predator was specializing in baboons and early humans. It is now clear that the hominids found in Dart's South African caves were not resident predators, but unfortunate victims. More a case of 'Man the hunted' than 'Man the hunter'.

Even today modern humans living in wilderness environments and without access to rifles are vulnerable to predators. Anthropologists recently estimated that among the Ache people of Amazonia, 6 per cent of deaths of young adults are due to jaguar predation. Other scientists have found documentary evidence of at least 393 people being killed or injured by lions, leopards and spotted hyenas in Uganda over an 80-year period ending recently. These modern human victims are substantially bigger than our early ancestors, have larger brains, are often armed, and live with greatly reduced predator populations, starkly illustrating the horrors our ancestors had to contend with.

Given this, we can imagine how Africa's megafauna has shaped not only our bodies but also our minds. Those millions of years we spent living in fear of carnivores perhaps explains phenomena as diverse as our

22ON DEADLY GROUND

27

PALAEO BALL GAMES

Our complex technology marks us out from other animals, but where did it come from? The first identifiable hominid tools date from about 2.5 million years ago. Before this time our tools were probably similar to those used by chimpanzees today – nut-cracking stones and wooden sticks for rooting out edible plants and invertebrates.

There is, however, another ancient, monster-inspired source for technological innovation that continues to entertain us even today. Primates have a long tradition of waving and even throwing sticks and stones to deter predator attacks; chimpanzees are occasionally observed using both methods to drive away leopards. Our ancestors' shift to walking upright freed their hands, allowing them to improve rock- and stick-throwing force and aim. It seems likely that early humans discovered stone and projectile technologies as a direct result of their need to drive away marauding predators. Those sticks and stones may have only later been adapted for scavenging and then hunting.

Today we are certainly the planet's best rock throwers, as a trip to any baseball or cricket match will demonstrate, though the defensive origin of our unique ball skills has long been forgotten.

▼ **Chimpanzees frequently use tools both to access food and in defence. Here they are using stone anvils and hammers to crack nuts.**

fear of the dark and our ability with ball-throwing games, and our fascination with zoos and monster movies.

The next step in stone-tool technology, and it was a big if relatively simple step, was to hit one rock (or bone) with another one to create sharp flakes and cores. Such simple implements may have first been created by accident – during nut-cracking, for example – but were soon being used to access previously unavailable foods.

The Human Vulture

Nature programmes on television frequently show vultures squabbling over carcasses, something we view with distaste. It is perhaps ironic that for much of our history we scavenged right alongside them, and it is likely that our ancestors would have viewed such scenes not with disgust but with relish. Technological innovation in the form of stone tools not only made early species of *Homo* more capable of defending themselves, but also changed our relationship with Earth's megafauna.

Animal bones and stone tools are first commonly found in association from about 2.5 million years ago. There are several theories about what these associations may mean. Could the clusters of bones and tools at places such as Olduvai and Koobi Fora in East Africa represent camps to

▼ Stone tools changed little over vast periods of time. The hand axes on the far left and right are 350,000 and 1 million years old, respectively.

which food was brought; were they the sites of hominid kills; or did these places simply contain the remains of animals that our ancestors had scavenged? Judging by their tools, the latter seems more likely. There is no evidence that these stone tools were used on spears or arrows, and hunting Africa's dangerous megafauna at close quarters with such artefacts would have been suicidal. It is conceivable that these stone edges were used to make perishable wooden hunting spears, but as yet there is no evidence of damage to animals from such weapons. *Homo erectus* from about 1.8 million years ago was probably incapable of hunting megafauna habitually, but that didn't stop hominids from scavenging carcasses they found.

Today many carnivores, including leopards, cheetahs and even lions, can be forced to abandon a kill when challenged by a group of hyenas. It seems logical to suppose that our ancestors, having learnt to repel predators, would follow the hyenas' example and begin to drive predators off their kills. But there is at least one important difference between hyenas and humans. Hyenas have sharp teeth for opening hides and other specialized teeth for crushing bones, and we do not. It may seem odd, but it would have been difficult for early humans to extract useful nutrition from a carcass without such powerful tools. Animal hides are incredibly tough, which is why we wear them on our feet, and bones are difficult to crack until they can be disarticulated from the body of their owners. The newly invented stone flakes and sharpened cores would have been used like razors to slice through hides and tendons, providing access to edible materials like bone marrow and brain, which are often left behind by predators like big cats.

It is amazing to think that after sharpened stone flakes and cores had been invented, there were no major technological advances in their design or production for an incredible 1 million years, until *Homo erectus* invented the teardrop-shaped hand axe 1.5 million years ago. This lack of technological advancement is unimaginable to us now and illustrates just how far from us these pre-humans were in their mental ability. If you recognize a division between people and animals, even *Homo erectus* was still an animal.

The Worm Turns

Evidence that large animals played an increasingly important part in the diet of *Homo erectus* comes from studies of the latter's teeth, which show a pattern of wear very different from that in earlier hominids. This change coincides with another strand of evidence: the first butchering marks on bone by stone tools. Stone tools seem to have been used to strip meat from carcasses and to cut through tendons and ligaments, allowing joints to be broken. Interestingly, in some cases it appears that *Homo erectus* had first access to the bones, because carnivore tooth marks appear on top of the marks made by stone tools. In other cases the tooth marks lie under the tools' marks, showing that the bones were scavenged by pre-humans.

It is intriguing that the largest extinction of African megafauna occurred in the early Pleistocene (1.7 million years ago), roughly coincident with the development of new stone-tool technology. Perhaps this ancient megafaunal extinction marks our shift from prey to predator, and the first major environmental impact of our line. If that is true, then in future we need to consider our deep past if we want to understand how we relate to nature.

Out of Africa

It took perhaps 3 million years for hominids to make their first tentative footsteps outside Africa, with *Homo erectus* leading the way 1.8 million years ago. By then our body and brain size had increased dramatically. A larger brain may explain why *Homo erectus* was the first of our ancestors to be able to cope with the more challenging climates of Eurasia.

Widespread invasion of Eurasia by pre-humans does not seem to have taken hold until about 800,000 years ago with *Homo erectus*; the brutal, ice-age climate of most of Europe probably prevented earlier colonization. But it was not only walking apes that were leaving Africa. Many of the animals that evolved in Africa alongside our ancestors also migrated

AFRICA

to Eurasia via the Near East in the late Pliocene (2–1.8 million years ago), along the same route as *Homo erectus*. Some animals, especially those that were able to swim, like the hippopotamus and elephant, may have made the journey by island-hopping across the Mediterranean from North Africa. The end result was that many of the animals that *Homo erectus* encountered in Asia and southern Europe were already familiar to hominids. In fact, pre-humans were probably unaware they had even left Africa. In Eurasia they met carnivorous species such as the hyena (*Pachycrocuta brevirostris*), the sabre-toothed cat (*Megantereon whitei*) and the dog (*Canis falconeri*). But now our ancestors were less attractive as prey, as a result of their new-found defensive abilities.

Around this time hominids probably paid special attention to hyenas. Working in highly coordinated packs, hyenas can both hunt successfully and steal carcasses from even the largest predators. They would have been formidable opponents and impressive role models to *Homo erectus*. However, our ancestors may have come off second best in any hyena encounter, since hominids still lacked effective, long-range weapons such as spears.

By about half a million years ago, several modern carnivore species invaded Eurasia from Africa. The giant hyenids were replaced by the

A MAN TO LOOK UP TO

Homo erectus was the first of our ancestors to explore the world beyond Africa. Increased brain size made them the first hominids to travel long distances, to make tools systematically, to have a home base where provisions were taken, and perhaps even to use fire. Travel beyond Africa was probably impossible for our ancestors until these characteristics had evolved – they were essential attributes for surviving the cold and dark winters of Eurasia.

Homo erectus was a highly successful species and thrived for more than 1.5 million years. Our own species, *Homo sapiens*, is a newcomer by comparison, having existed for perhaps only 200,000 years. Although we often make fun of our prehistoric ancestors, our own species has yet to prove itself as a long-term survivor. We have a lot to live up to.

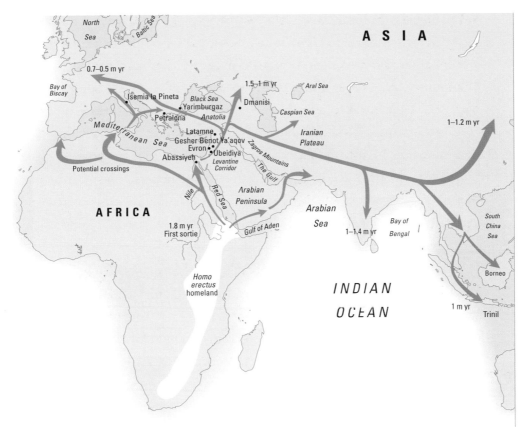

▲ Possible routes by which *Homo erectus* conquered Eurasia.

modern spotted hyena (*Crocuta crocuta*), while the lion and leopard (*Panthera pardus*) replaced the sabre-toothed cats. These faunal changes probably made scavenging more difficult for hominids – the new predators were able to consume more of their victims' bodies, leaving little behind for scavengers. Today the behaviour and even facial expressions of lions suggest that they view us primarily as competitors rather than prey. However, new species of deer, ox, rhino and horse in Europe may have provided new opportunities for pre-humans.

Chapter 3 investigates the first conquest of Eurasia by our species, but it is worth considering some of that evidence now, because at present there are more archaeological sites from the European borders of Africa for this period than from within Africa itself.

Monster Hunters

Recent discoveries of megafaunal bones in Europe have shown evidence of planned hunting and systematic butchery of large mammals by our ancestors from about half a million years ago. At Boxgrove, England, *Homo heidelbergensis*, a descendant of *Homo erectus*, butchered woolly rhinos, deer and horses. It also seems that these hominids were now equipped with more sophisticated weapons – one of the bones (the shoulder bone of a horse) has a hole that looks as if it was made by a spear. Amazingly some of the bones still contain fragments of the flint tools used during butchering. Such systematic hunting represents a dramatic change for our ancestors – far from being defenceless prey, they were now among the top predators of their world. At Schöningen, Germany, a site dating to 400,000 years ago shows not only the bones of our megafaunal prey, but also the tools with which they were killed. Wooden artefacts preserved at the site include a double-ended spear, probably used for stabbing animals at close quarters, and several throwing spears about 2 m (6½ feet) long and weighted like modern javelins. These may have been used for killing from a safer distance.

Schöningen shows that early hominids of Europe were capable of killing small and medium-sized herbivores, but what about the biggest animals? Most of the early evidence of hominids hunting mammoths, elephants, rhinos and bison has been disputed as collections of bones and stone tools brought together by chance. But, at Arridos in Spain, our ancestors do appear to have butchered elephants 300,000 years ago. More evidence, dating to 180,000 years ago, can be seen at La Cotte in St Brelade's Bay, Jersey, where two piles of mammoth and rhino bones were found in a deep deposit under a headland. The bones appear to be the remains of animals driven off a cliff, perhaps on two separate occasions. One pile contains eleven mammoths and three woolly rhinos, while the other contains seven mammoths and two rhinos. With the mammoths weighing about 2 tons, and the rhinos about 1 ton, it is clear that there was far more meat than a group of hominids could consume or process. If the interpretation of this site in Jersey is correct, it means that at least

▲ Prehistoric art frequently documents the conflict between humans and Earth's megafauna.

This African rock painting illustrates a man hunting an elephant.

occasional mass slaughter of megafauna began earlier than we had previously thought.

It is only recently that we have come to realize the disturbing possibility that the rise and dispersal of humans (*Homo sapiens*) may have caused the extinction of other members of our family. Through nearly all of our 5-million-year history a number of species of hominid have coexisted. For example, in Africa several different types of *Australopithecus* shared the continent not only with other members of their genus, but also with the first member of our own genus, *Homo*, which then replaced them. Later *Homo habilis* and *Homo rudolfensis* overlapped in time, as did *Homo erectus*. Most recently *Homo sapiens* and Neanderthals (*Homo neanderthalensis*) collided in Europe, perhaps until as recently as 35,000 years ago. Most palaeontologists now believe that our species either outcompeted or directly exterminated our Neanderthal cousins. Today there is only one human species left on the planet: our own. This is not a trivial historical footnote but instead perhaps a revealing insight into our nature, for it may be one of the earliest signals from the past showing that we are capable of exterminating, either directly or indirectly, Earth's large animals. Even when those creatures are our cousins.

▲ Skulls of two species of extinct australopithecines. Many types of human monster once roamed the Earth – now there is only one.

The Last Human Monster

Few people are aware of how remarkably recent our species (*Homo sapiens*) is. Anatomically modern humans first appear in the fossil record only about 200,000 years ago. Today there are two major schools of thought as to where and how we first evolved. Multiregionalists believe that the various *Homo erectus* populations in Africa and Eurasia evolved into *Homo sapiens*, whereas 'Out of Africa' proponents believe modern humans evolved within Africa and only later spread out across the world, replacing other human species. This question matters because it could help us understand the amount of time that the megafauna beyond Africa may have had to adapt to us.

So which was it? Multiregionalism predicts simultaneous evolution throughout the Old World, requiring constant gene flow between Africa, Europe and Asia, sustained by frequent migrations and interbreeding between populations of *Homo erectus* and their descendants. Supporters of the 'Out of Africa' theory, such as palaeontologist Chris Stringer of the Natural History Museum, London, point out that the fossil record shows no evidence of the intermediate species that would have existed if *Homo erectus* had evolved into modern humans outside Africa. The oldest fossils of modern humans have been found in Africa, suggesting an African origin for our species. Furthermore, the strong similarity between modern human populations suggests a recent common ancestor. As a result, 'Out of Africa' proponents argue that modern humans evolved in Africa and migrated to the rest of the world only recently.

Scientists have turned to genetics to try to resolve this debate. By counting the number of mutations that have built up over time in different human populations, they can now estimate how long it is since our most recent common ancestor lived. Rather than studying the whole human genome, the scientists examined a type of DNA called mitochondrial DNA, or mtDNA. Mutations occur more frequently in mtDNA, making it useful for tracing evolution over recent history. Surprisingly, scientists have found very little variation in the mtDNA of humans throughout the world — less than a tenth of the variation seen in just one species of chimpanzee. This suggests that all modern humans are very closely related and share a common ancestor who lived perhaps only 200,000 years ago. Also, mtDNA is most varied among African people, implying that they have been accumulating mutations for longest, and therefore represent the oldest modern human populations. These results strongly favour the 'Out of Africa' theory and suggest that we replaced all other existing members of the hominid family. Exactly why the other hominids disappeared is a mystery. Perhaps there was conflict between species, or maybe the other hominids could not compete with us and died out gradually. Either way it seems that there was little interbreeding between the different species, because our DNA shows remarkably little variation today.

▼ All modern humans belong to the species *Homo sapiens*. Competition with other hominid species, as well as adaptation to new environments and animals, shaped our minds and bodies.

Revolution in the Black Hole

If the appearance of *Homo sapiens* happened a shockingly recent 200,000 years ago, what is even more disturbing is that the present archaeological evidence suggests that it took a further 100,000 years before we became 'behaviourally' human. For most of our history, technological innovation has occurred at a glacial pace, and tools are remarkably uniform throughout vast expanses of our range and time, something that is unthinkable today. As Jared Diamond has pointed out, aliens visiting Earth before about 100,000 years ago would have seen human technology as being little more sophisticated than that of sea otters, chimps, Galápagos finches and many other animals.

All that may have changed quite suddenly in what has been termed the 'Upper Palaeolithic revolution', which marks the point when we became truly human. Before this point we were just another species of big animal; after it we created technological and cultural diversity and innovation on a grand scale. But the archaeological and fossil record for the crucial period – around 100,000 years ago – is so weak that it has been called a 'black hole'. Yet it is in that time that we became what we are now. Future researchers lucky enough to find excavation sites from this period will help us to determine how and why we were transformed.

Recent finds suggest that the revolution began in Africa, but again the best sites are found in the better-studied Europe, where *Homo sapiens* began to create a new range of artefacts, called the Aurignacian tools. Suddenly, across much of Europe, around 100 tools with marked regional variations arrive, in contrast to the uniformity of earlier times. Another first for the Upper Palaeolithic was the greater frequency of tools made of bone, ivory and antlers – materials that produced better harpoons, needles and projectile weapons.

Some of the Aurignacian artefacts were so fine and delicate that they were almost transparent and would have been of no practical use. These objects probably had artistic value or ritual significance. Their appearance represents an important step forward in the mental development of our ancestors, making them people we would identify with.

Radical cultural changes coincided with the increasing complexity of tools. The sites that humans inhabited became much larger, and instead of living in caves or rock shelters, they began to favour settlements on open land. Evidence for long-distance contact, and perhaps trade, is suggested by the presence of exotic shells and stones far from their site of origin. Even musical instruments, such as pipes and flutes made from bone, made an appearance. Innovation was rapid during the Upper Palaeolithic, and by about 30,000 years ago cave painting and art had become established traditions in Europe at least. Although Neanderthals may have had some artistic expression, it was not as rich or detailed as that of our ancestors from the same period. Could it be just a coincidence that the new, more sophisticated form of art appeared shortly after modern humans arrived in Eurasia?

Africa's Living Monsters

From the time of the first hominids some 5 million years ago to the evolution of our own species, *Homo sapiens*, a few tens of thousands of years ago, hominids have had a uniquely long and complex relationship with the megafauna of Africa. Nowhere else have hominids and megafauna coexisted for so long. As a result Africa's animals have had millions of years to coevolve with us, to track our various technological and behavioural advances and adapt to them. Africa's animals are different from those on the rest of the planet simply because they have had the longest period in which to get to know us. It is perhaps not surprising that they have a deep and long-standing mistrust of humans. Even today, people in Africa are not only at risk from the world's most dangerous carnivores, but also may be attacked by Earth's largest and most aggressive herbivores. When threatened, Africa's large animals seem to charge first and ask questions later, and this has probably saved them from the fate of monsters elsewhere. That is why people go on safari holidays to Kenya and not Quebec – Africa is the home of the streetwise survivors.

▲ Africa's living monsters are streetwise survivors that, when threatened, charge first and ask questions later. Rhinoceros injure and kill more people every year than lions do.

The gradual development of bigger brains and better tools eventually gave our ancestors protection from Africa's carnivores, but this change did not bode well for other animals. They found themselves at risk from a new predator, and one that hunted in well-coordinated packs. Over time the African herbivores evolved defences against their new enemies, becoming stronger, bigger, faster and more violent.

When hominids first left Africa, many of the animals they encountered in the bordering land had themselves come from Africa. The mammoths and rhinos of Europe had evolved from African ancestors, for instance. It may be that partly shared past that gave Europe's megafauna some protection from the human race. In more distant lands, such as Australia, Earth's monsters would not be so lucky.

2

AUSTRALIA

● 68,000 years ago

Thousands of years before Captain Cook arrived in Australia the ancestors of today's Aborigines made a daring sea voyage to an astonishing world populated by monstrous marsupials, giant reptiles and huge flightless birds, all of which lived in a land ruled by fire and drought.

◄ On arrival in Australia people discovered the only continent in the world where marsupials were the dominant form of mammal. Red kangaroos would have been a strange sight.

A World Apart

Australia is truly a world apart. This, the smallest of Earth's continents, was isolated by continental drift from all other landmasses for 45 million years. Cut off from the rest of the planet, a bizarre flora and fauna evolved, making the continent seem ancient and alien in comparison with its neighbours.

As Australia underwent its long isolation, the world's climate became cooler and drier. This global cooling acted in concert with the continent's long drift northwards towards warmer latitudes and forced a change from

▲ Mulga trees (*Acacia*) in a desert landscape. The interior of Australia has become increasingly arid through time and plants like the acacias have adapted to the changes.

Australia's original dense, broad-leaved forests to drier, more open woodland, grassland and desert. Drought-resistant trees such as *Eucalyptus* and *Acacia*, as well as the tough *Spinifex* grasses, began to dominate. About 6 million years ago, climate change within Australia intensified, increasing the aridity even further. Finally, as the Pleistocene Ice age dawned – and locked away much of the world's water in the huge polar ice caps – the savagely dry climate secured the supremacy of fire-resistant plants.

The End of Isolation

The only way to reach Australia has always been across the open sea. In prehistory Australia and New Guinea were actually a single landmass known as Greater Australia. Although Greater Australia and Southeast Asia eventually became close neighbours, they were still separated by water, and travel to Australia has always been a treacherous journey across open ocean. Even in times of lowest sea level, the crossing was never less than 60–100 km (37–62 miles). Flying creatures and ocean-going swimmers could easily travel from one shoreline to the other, but for land animals it was perilous: they would have had to float across on tree trunks or other drifting vegetation. Only small creatures were likely to be carried as passengers on such rafts. Of the thousands of potential animal colonists that accidentally floated out to sea, a tiny fraction would actually make a safe landing and become successful animal pioneers.

THE LOST CONTINENT

An accurate map of the world is a very fleeting thing, geologically speaking. Maps are mere snapshots of a world in motion, because the shape, size and position of the continents changes over time. Earth's crust is made up of plates moved slowly about by currents in the underlying molten mantle. Continents collide and coalesce into larger 'supercontinents' or are ripped apart and scattered across the surface of the globe. A continent that was at the poles at one given moment may be at the equator 100 million years later.

Until the beginning of the Cretaceous period, Australia was part of the ancient supercontinent Pangaea. When Pangaea broke apart, an Australian–Antarctic landmass was created. Australia finally split from Antarctica 45 million years ago, although a shallow sea separated the two continents for several million years prior to this. Australia drifted north, its fauna and flora evolving in complete isolation until about 25–15 million years ago, when the continent neared the islands of Southeast Asia. Animals could then begin to make the perilous journey between the two landmasses. The meeting of these creatures and their evolution together over the next few million years gave Australia a truly unique fauna.

▲ The ancestors of mice like the Mitchell's hopping mouse (*Notomys mitchelli*) would have made the journey by raft from Southeast Asia to Australia about 15 million years ago.

Despite the overwhelming odds, a number of animals did survive that dangerous journey. Many Australian birds and small marsupials migrated west to islands such as Timor and Sulawesi. However, only three types of placental mammal travelled in the opposite direction: bats, rats and mice. The bats obviously flew, while about 15 million years ago the rodents made a sea voyage. All of the numerous other placental mammals found in Australia today – including the dingo – are latecomers introduced by either the Aborigines or subsequent Asian and European explorers.

A Passage from India

The first people to reach Australia also made a sea crossing from Asia: the final stage of a long journey from humanity's birthplace. Modern humans expanded out of Africa about 200,000 years ago (see Chapter 1). At that time, northern Eurasia's climate was too harsh for habitation by people without special technological and social innovations (see Chapter 3). These first African migrants must have felt more at home along the warm shores of Asia.

Evidence suggests that modern humans reached mainland Southeast Asia as early as 90,000 years ago. Then, as now, the region was covered in rainforest. Fossil pollen from Sumatra and Java reveals both lowland and highland forest even when the coolest and driest of Ice-age climates caused the demise of similar forests in Greater Australia. The thick rainforests prevented animals that prefer open country (camels, horses and giraffes) from invading Southeast Asia.

Southeast Asia's rainforests were a test-bed for human adaptability and a training ground for the invasion of Australia. Jungles and other dense forests are – contrary to popular belief – very difficult places for hunter-gatherers to make a living. So if rainforests are such a bad bet, why did humans enter Southeast Asia at all? The answer is that the region had rich coastal environments that offered plentiful food. Such resources would have been safer and easier to harvest than those in the tropical forests, so perhaps the people who colonized Southeast Asia made most of their living from the sea, supplemented with a little inland hunting of small to medium-sized game. The animals they encountered are known from fossils found in Niah Cave in Borneo and from various sites in the Pandang highlands of Sumatra. Of these, monkeys, pigs, wild cattle, tapirs, antelopes and deer were all likely prey for those first hunters. Not on the menu, but sharing their lands, were orang-utans, various species of elephant and rhino, a Southeast Asian hippo, leopards, tigers and the sun bear.

It is worth noting that the original people of coastal Asia probably looked more like modern Australian Aborigines than like present-day

EGGS, POUCHES AND BOUNCING BABIES

What type of mammal are you? It all depends on how you give birth. Monotreme mammals, such as the platypus and echidna, lay eggs. After the young hatch, they suckle for milk like all mammals. Marsupials and placental mammals (such as human beings) give birth to live young. But even the biggest of marsupial mothers delivers a tiny, underdeveloped baby that has to spend a long time growing in the safety of her pouch, nourished by milk. Placental babies, on the other hand, do all this development in the womb, where they are sustained by a large placenta. Even placental youngsters that are born hairless and blind (like kittens) are large and sturdy in comparison with their marsupial cousins.

▼ **Even when quite large, young red kangaroos will return to the safety of their mother's pouch for food and shelter.**

Oriental people, who are relatively recent arrivals from further north. Even today, small populations of dark-skinned, curly-haired hunter-gatherers with genetic links to the native peoples of New Guinea and Australia still live in places like Sri Lanka, the Malay Peninsula and the Andaman Islands. Such people are the descendants of the first explorers.

As people swept towards Australia, they successively discovered and colonized the small islands to the east of Bali. These islands lacked large, warm-blooded predators like tigers and leopards. Despite the presence of the Komodo dragon and its relatives in Indonesia, the islands were a relatively safe haven for humanity. People settled there and continued to explore the surrounding seas until about 68,000 years ago, when a momentous event occurred – someone discovered Australia.

Walkabout on Water

There are two likely routes for the first journey to Australia. The first involves island-hopping down through Indonesia, passing through Java, Bali, Lombok and other islands of the Lesser Sundas, the last of which is Timor. From there it was one final sea voyage across the Timor Sea to either the Kimberley in northwest Australia or Arnhem Land at the tip of the Northern Territory. Even with lowered sea levels, this last crossing was a challenging 87 km (54 miles). However, experimental raft-building and computer simulations of tides and currents prove that in the monsoon season, any rafts blown away from the coast of Timor inevitably end up on Australian shores. Most rafts complete the journey in 7–10 days – an unpleasant but survivable trip.

The alternative route is a voyage from Borneo to Sulawesi, and then to island-hop across the Molucca and Seram Seas to New Guinea. After arriving in New Guinea the travellers could simply walk across the land bridge to Australia, arriving in Cape York, Queensland. The shortest sea journey on this route would have been 60 km (37 miles).

The fact that the first Australians were the only large species successfully to make the perilous sea voyage tells us something important.

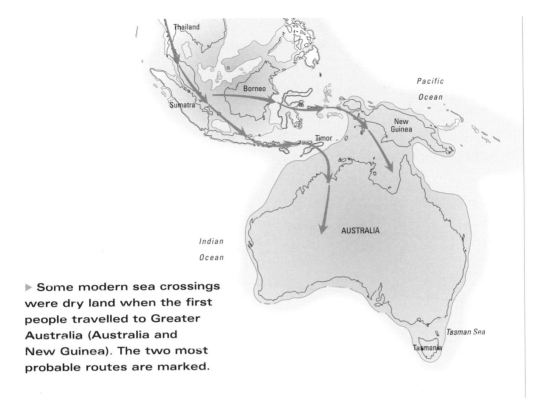

▶ Some modern sea crossings were dry land when the first people travelled to Greater Australia (Australia and New Guinea). The two most probable routes are marked.

SEA LEVEL AND LAND BRIDGES

During the Ice age, people could walk across many areas that are today covered by sea. Because much of the world's water was trapped in vast polar ice caps, sea level was lowered, creating new lands for plants and animals to invade. Sometimes this newly uncovered ground formed 'land bridges' between previously unconnected places. Seventy thousand years ago sea level was 68–75 m (223–246 feet) lower than today. Although the increase in land area meant that much of the journey from Southeast Asia to Greater Australia could be made on foot, there were still several substantial sea barriers to cross.

We do not know whether the first voyagers made their journey at a time of normal or low sea level. Obviously, the lower the sea level, the shorter the sea crossing. On the other hand, in times of normal sea levels the currents and monsoon winds are more favourable for the voyage, promoting southward and eastward travel towards Australia. Rising sea levels have been proposed as the trigger that drove humans to move from Southeast Asia: as habitable land was drowned by the advancing waters, groups of people may have moved onwards in search of new islands.

These people weren't just accidental castaways, like the tiny rats and mice that preceded them. Neither were they like the anatomically modern but mentally ape-like *Homo sapiens* that were the first examples of our species in Africa and the Near East. Rather, the first Australians were sophisticated people with modern brains, a complex culture and the skills to plan, build, sail and navigate an ocean-going craft to a specific destination.

THE DATING GAME

The exact timing of human arrival in Australia is hotly debated. Humans got there at least 50,000 years ago, and some scientists believe the true date lies as far back as 80,000. Why such discrepancies? Part of the problem is radiocarbon dating. This compares the ratio of radioactive carbon-14 to the normal carbon-12 in a sample of once-living material like bone or wood. The radioactive carbon is unstable and decays over time, so the smaller the proportion of carbon-14 in an item, the older that object is. It is a marvellous tool for archaeology. However, for very ancient sites, radiocarbon has a limitation: the technique is accurate only for materials that are less than 37,000 years old. It can be stretched to analyze objects up to 10,000 years older than this, but by this stage there is so little carbon-14 in the samples that any contamination with other carbon can lead to large inaccuracies. Any date beyond 40,000 years ago is best interpreted as meaning 'at least 40,000 years old, possibly much

older'. Some researchers believe that any dates older than 35,000 years have to be taken with a pinch of salt.

The first Australians seem to have arrived before 37,000 years ago, so the crucial period of exploration and settlement is beyond the range of radiocarbon dating. Palaeontologists and archaeologists are attempting to resolve this problem by turning to other techniques for dating fossils and artefacts. New methods have been devised, like electron spin resonance and optically stimulated luminescence dating. They too have limitations – and their very recent development means we are still not sure what all the limitations are – but they are constantly being tested and refined. The best way to get a date for an artefact or site is to apply as many techniques to it as possible and compare all the results. However, this is an expensive and time-consuming business. If Australia's pioneers had arrived later, life would be much simpler for archaeologists.

Various types of watercraft have been suggested for the sea crossings. The very first people to reach Australia certainly had the technological capability to construct bark canoes, reed or bark-bundle boats, and rafts. The most likely choice is the raft, as they are more seaworthy on long voyages. The Aborigines of northwestern Australia, in historical times, sometimes used mangrove wood rafts to travel as far as 16 km (10 miles) in treacherous seas.

Our voyagers may even have known that Australia was out there before they set off. The coast of Ice-age Australia was visible to people on the islands of Halmahera and Gebe in the northern Moluccas. Bushfires on the Australian mainland can be spotted from even further away, as the smoke rises several thousand metres into the air and can be seen by someone on a beach more than 110 km (68 miles) distant. So even people on faraway Timor were aware that there was land to the south of them.

The existence of land out there wasn't news to the first voyagers. However, it would have been a great shock to discover the extent of the new country, the monstrous animals within it and the total lack of human inhabitants.

How Many Made the Trip?

Some Aboriginal legends speak of only a few travellers making the first voyage: a man and his sisters, or a single mythological being. Popular culture often depicts only a small number of people staggering ashore — a romanticized *Swiss Family Robinson* for Australia. However, tiny groups of random castaways would be prone to getting wiped out without leaving any descendants. To sustain a viable colony, a lot of people had to reach Australia. It is likely that many different groups of travellers made the voyage — a few by accident, but most on deliberate and organized expeditions in search of new lands. Indeed, people may even have made return journeys to Southeast Asia with news of their discovery, and thus prompted further explorers to set out. Gradually the population of the landfall areas would have swelled, with the arrival of new migrants as

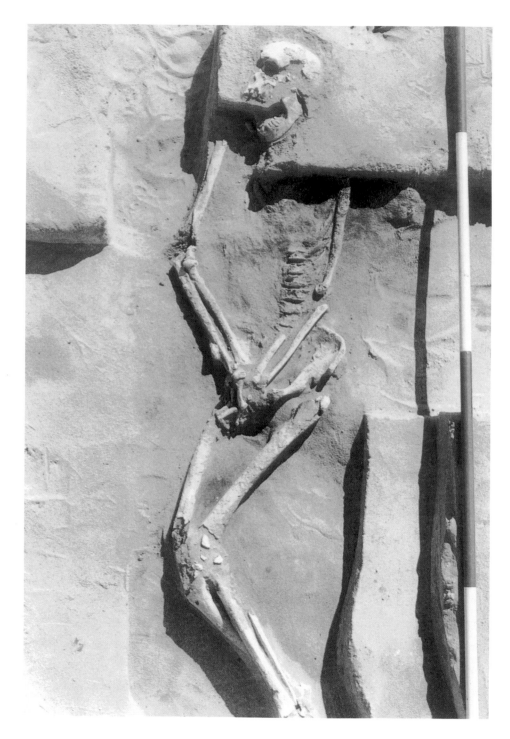

▲ The skeleton known as Mungo III was discovered in 1974 at the dried-up lake bed called Lake Mungo. It is currently the oldest known burial in Australia.

well as babies born there. As the region grew more crowded, people would have moved along the coast or inland in search of unoccupied territory.

This first colonization of Australia was perhaps akin to European settlers gradually moving from east to west across the Americas. While a few colonists advanced the frontier, others began to settle and make claims on particular stretches of land. But there was one major difference – the frontier ahead of our pioneers was always empty. Prehistoric Australia had no indigenous people to be displaced.

The World's Most Dated Man

One of the most important pieces of evidence for early arrival of humans in Australia is a burial found by geologist Jim Bowler at Lake Mungo in the Willandra Lakes region of New South Wales. The skeleton – known as Mungo III – is probably a male with chronic arthritis in the right elbow. His teeth are worn down in a way that suggests that he used them to strip plant fibre for cord and netting. His body was covered in red ochre, which must have been carried in from elsewhere as this mineral is not available locally.

Mungo III was originally dated to between 28,000 and 32,000 years ago using radiocarbon dating, but recently Professor Ranier Grun of the Australian National University at Canberra has applied a range of new techniques to the burial and the surrounding sediments, and recorded dates ranging from 50,000 to 81,000 years ago. The best estimate from combining all these results is that Mungo III is between 50,000 and 68,000 years old. Because he died in New South Wales, his burial must have occurred many years after the very first people set foot in northern Australia. It likely took around 1,000 to 3,000 years to colonize the whole continent, so Mungo III tells us that the first Australians made landfall at least 51,000 to 71,000 years ago. Many scientists favour a figure of about 65,000 to 68,000 years ago for the timing of that first step on to Australia's shores. What the new colonists encountered when they arrived there was extraordinary.

DIPROTODON

Diprotodon optatum was the biggest marsupial ever. It stood just a fraction shorter than a white rhinoceros but weighed a little more. The largest were a massive 2–2.5 tons, their smaller relatives weighing a mere 1 ton. It was originally believed that there were many species of *Diprotodon* of varying size, but it now seems more probable that the 2-ton giants were males and the 1-ton lightweights were females. A big male *Diprotodon* stood 1.7 m (5½ feet) high at the shoulder and measured about 3 m (10 feet) from nose to tail; the skull alone was almost a metre (3 feet) long.

To make its huge head lighter, *Diprotodon* had large, empty spaces in its skull, like an elephant has. The skull had almost a double structure, with an outer layer of bone to which the massive jaw muscles were attached, and an inner layer to hold and protect the brain. But whereas elephants have a relatively large brain within their massive skull, *Diprotodon*'s brain was small.

Diprotodon was the most common of Pleistocene Australia's large herbivores. Females have even been found with the remains of babies in their pouch, and fossilized footprints were found at Lake Callabonna in southern Australia. The footprints have impressions

▲ The first human pioneers in Australia discovered herds of giant marsupials like *Diprotodon*.

of fur around the foot, so we know that *Diprotodon* was hairy like a horse, not bald like a rhino. The footprints also tell us that *Diprotodon* did not walk or trot like a rhino, but paced like a camel does – moving both feet on one side of its body at the same time. The creator of the tracks at Lake Callabonna was travelling at a leisurely 8–9 km/h (5–6 miles/h). *Diprotodon* could put on a short burst of greater speed to escape from danger, but it was not built to be a long-distance runner.

Also from Lake Callabonna are *Diprotodon* skeletons with the remains of their last meal in the stomach – before they died they had been eating saltbush. This tough plant is not a decent meal, so perhaps these *Diprotodon* were desperate. They may have been dying of starvation during a drought.

56

Alien Australia

Australia's mammals hail from ancient lineages. With the exception of rats and mice, all of Australia's native mammals are marsupials or egg-laying monotremes. Modern Australia is almost devoid of large native mammals – except for a few kangaroos – but in prehistory it boasted a much more spectacular fauna. There was a whole range of marsupials and monotremes that are now extinct: carnivorous rat kangaroos, giant wombats and giant echidnas, to name but a few. These long-vanished creatures varied in size from a 5-kg (11-lb) rat kangaroo to monsters of over a ton (*Diprotodon*). The only marsupials in Southeast Asia are small creatures like phalangers. The first Aborigines must have been astonished by the sight of hopping kangaroos and slow-moving giants such as *Diprotodon*.

Monstrous marsupials were not the only wonders in store for the new arrivals. Australia boasted giant flightless birds – cassowaries, emus and

▲ *Diprotodon optatum* weighed more than 2 tons, making it the largest marsupial ever to have lived. It was found throughout Australia (except Tasmania) and became extinct some time between 45,000 and 25,000 years ago.

huge geese nicknamed the 'demon ducks of doom' – as well as the enormous predatory reptile *Megalania*.

The landscape of Australia 71,000–51,000 years ago was also a surprise to our human voyagers. Instead of the familiar rainforests of home, they found savannah and 'dry jungle' covering the exposed flatlands of the continental shelf. The very flat terrain was prone to regular flooding, so some areas were covered in grass-like sedges. Patches of trees dotted the grassland here and there – mainly *Eucalyptus*, *Callitris* and

THE MARSUPIAL LION

Australia's largest mammalian predator was the marsupial lion (*Thylacoleo carnifex*). In appearance and habits it had many similarities to the big cats, such as retractable claws; hence its common name. But the marsupial lion had a trick up its sleeve not possessed by placental cats – the 'thumb' of the forepaw bore a huge and deadly curved claw, much larger than all its others. The action of this thumb claw is not fully understood, but it might have been a killing tool for inflicting deep wounds – in the way that the dinosaur *Velociraptor* (made famous by the film *Jurassic Park*) used the enlarged claws on its hind feet to kill.

Even more remarkable were the marsupial lion's teeth. Instead of the large canine teeth typical of placental carnivores, it had enlarged incisors, giving it a comical bucktoothed appearance. Its molars had very long, blade-like edges that sheared past each other to slice efficiently through flesh. Huge jaw muscles provided

▲ Like true cats, the marsupial lion had retractable claws, but instead of large canine teeth, its killing tools were its enlarged incisors.

the power for this fearsome bite.

Its total length from nose to tail was just short of 1.8 m (6 feet). Recent estimates put its weight at 70–150 kg (154–331 lb) – equivalent to that of a jaguar or a large wolf. But with its chunky stature the marsupial lion was much more 'butch' than even the sturdiest of jaguars. It had a very cat-like pelvis, adapted for running, crouching, stalking and pouncing. The marsupial lion's powerful but flexible forelimbs could rotate in the way a cat can rotate its paws, or in the way we can rotate our hands.

Casuarina. There were also swathes of denser woodland – dry deciduous forest and vine-thicket communities, where grass was scarce. Grazing animals such as red kangaroos ruled the savannah, while browsing animals thrived in the vine-thicket forests.

The largest mammal predator present when humans arrived in Australia was the marsupial lion (*Thylacoleo carnifex*). Older reconstructions of this animal depict it as a tree-living predator, lurking on overhead branches and jumping on unsuspecting animals that passed below. This image is based on Victorian misconceptions of how leopards hunt antelopes. In fact, the marsupial lion stalked its prey on the ground in true big-cat fashion. However, it might have hauled its kill up into a tree to keep it out of the reach of scavengers, as leopards do today. While a leopard hopes to deter hyenas and lions, *Thylacoleo* sought to defend its meals from the marsupial wolf (*Thylacinus*) and the giant ripper lizard (*Megalania*).

Palaeontologists puzzled over *Thylacoleo* prey, some even suggesting that it ate melons and other fruit. Eventually, marsupial lion toothmarks were discovered on the bones of megafauna such as *Diprotodon* at Lancefield Swamp, near Melbourne. But were these giant herbivores

LANCEFIELD SWAMP

Lancefield Swamp near Melbourne is an impressive bone accumulation around an ancient spring. The site is about 26,000 years old and contains the remains of up to 10,000 animals, including extinct megafauna such as *Diprotodon*, *Genyornis* and *Macropus titan* – the large ancestor of the eastern grey kangaroo. Strange marks on some of the bones were made by the teeth of the marsupial lion, *Thylacoleo*. It has been suggested that many – if not all – of these animals died during a drought. Stone tools were also found, but it is unclear if they are the same age as the bones. Future studies may unravel the secret history of Lancefield Swamp.

◀ **The cuts and gouges on this grey kangaroo's leg bone were inflicted by the teeth of the marsupial lion.**

killed or simply scavenged once they were already dead? We do have one skeleton that gives us an answer: a juvenile *Nototherium* (a relative of *Diprotodon*) from Tasmania, which appears to have escaped from the fearsome predator. One of the animal's hind limbs was injured by the marsupial lion's teeth, but the victim survived long enough for the bone to begin healing.

Would the marsupial lion have been a threat to the first Australians? If it attacked giants like the two-ton *Diprotodon*, it was certainly big and powerful enough to tackle a human. Sadly, we have no evidence to tell us whether the marsupial lion hunted humans or was hunted by them – or if both sides learned to keep a healthy distance. But it is hard to imagine being able to sleep soundly with this creature around.

The marsupial lion's main competitor for the position of top predator was the giant reptile *Megalania*. After the demise of the dinosaurs, several

THE RIPPER

Megalania prisca – the giant ripper lizard – was the largest lizard that ever lived. It was the Komodo dragon writ large. While the Komodo dragon can grow up to 3 m (10 feet) long, *Megalania* reached a maximum length of about 5.5 m (18 feet) and weighed an impressive 400 kg (882 lb).

Megalania's closest living relative is the perentie (*Varanus giganteus*), but being much larger, *Megalania* was probably more similar to the Komodo dragon in lifestyle and eating habits. Like the Komodo, it hunted by day, even in the worst wet-season downpours. After dark it became less active and rested under trees, using the shelter of the canopy to minimize heat loss during the cool nights.

Komodo dragons are known to prey upon people, so the first Australians may have discovered that they were on *Megalania*'s menu. The hunting strategy of a Komodo is simple: try to smash the prey to the ground and tear it to pieces. The armoury needed to accomplish this feat includes powerful claws and a wicked set of large, curved and serrated teeth. If a Komodo fails to kill in the first attack, a secret weapon comes into play: its saliva is full of dangerous bacteria that cause any wounds to fester and go septic. The Komodo follows the stricken animal and either waits for it to die or attacks it again in its weakened state. It is likely that *Megalania* also possessed this bacterial trick.

If *Megalania* perceived the world

lineages of giant predatory reptiles arose in the tropics. *Megalania* and its close relation the Komodo dragon were relative latecomers, evolutionarily speaking, but as such they overlapped in time with people. Encounters between the first Australians and *Megalania* were the closest experience that humanity has ever had to dealing with a dinosaur.

Large predators need large prey to sustain them. The prey of these carnivores was a variety of medium- to large-sized grazers and browsers. Some, like the kangaroos and emu, are familiar to us today. Others are long since extinct. Australia's dry and unproductive nature meant that it never boasted the teeming herds seen in places like the Serengeti (wildebeest, zebra) or the American Great Plains (bison). Instead, the big grazers and browsers formed small groups, in herds of perhaps only a few dozen. But, small herds or not, these odd creatures would have been an amazing sight to the first Australians.

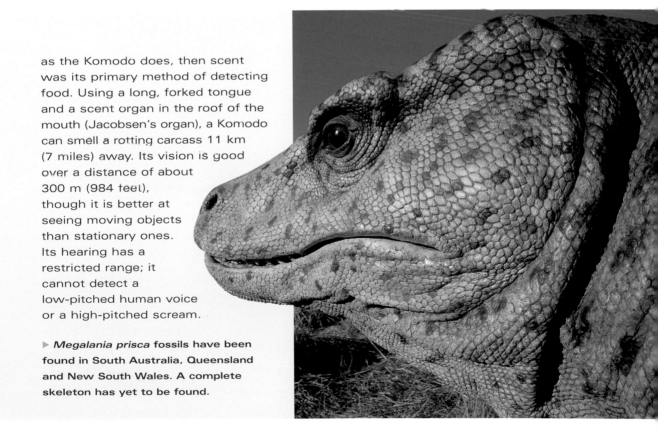

as the Komodo does, then scent was its primary method of detecting food. Using a long, forked tongue and a scent organ in the roof of the mouth (Jacobsen's organ), a Komodo can smell a rotting carcass 11 km (7 miles) away. Its vision is good over a distance of about 300 m (984 feet), though it is better at seeing moving objects than stationary ones. Its hearing has a restricted range; it cannot detect a low-pitched human voice or a high-pitched scream.

▶ *Megalania prisca* fossils have been found in South Australia, Queensland and New South Wales. A complete skeleton has yet to be found.

The First Australians

One of the main skills of *Homo sapiens* is our ability to adapt to new places and new diets. This resourcefulness enabled the first Australians to overcome many challenges and claim Greater Australia as their home. One major obstacle would have been the more seasonal climate – north Australia has a long dry season in the winter. The colonists quickly learned that pools were a valuable aid to hunting. Because water sources are short-lived or scattered, animals are tied to water holes and thus predictable in their movements. This is of great advantage to hunters.

In their old lands, our explorers were more used to catching small game than to tackling large animals, although perhaps they occasionally hunted creatures like the elephant *Stegodon* on Sulawesi. Once in Australia, they would have been confronted by a much more diverse and peculiar megafauna. Did they change their hunting techniques to cope with larger (and thus potentially more dangerous) prey? Or did they continue to hunt small- and medium-sized game, learning how to catch wallabies and emus? We look to archaeology to answer these questions, but the archaeological record for this period is rather sparse, for a number of reasons.

Hunter-gatherers have a very mobile lifestyle, migrating from place to place within their territory. Their possessions need to be lightweight, preferably multipurpose, and not numerous or bulky, so that they can be easily carried on a day's walk. It is impractical for hunter-gatherers to own many possessions, and the ability to travel quickly and effortlessly is vital in a land with little water. Archaeologists studying ancient hunter-gatherers look with jealousy at the wealth of objects retrieved from their colleagues' excavations of farms or villages. In Australia there are even fewer artefacts than usual, because the acid and sandy soils destroy organic material such as wood and bone.

Non-perishable items like stone tools are thus the most commonly found artefacts. These early stone implements were not very sophisticated in design. Many were used to manufacture and maintain wooden tools

STEREOTYPES OF THE STONE AGE

Many people have a vision of hunter-gatherers as the ultimate sexist lifestyle, with men conducting grand hunts and reaping the rewards, while women work back at camp, collecting plants and doing housework. In reality, men gather as well as hunt, and women hunt as well as gather. For example, when out on long-range hunting trips, Alyawara Aborigine men often collect bush potato (*Ipomoea costata*) and native tomato (*Solanum*). But while hunter-gatherer men usually gather to feed themselves as they go about their daily business, women gather to feed their whole family. Usually women provide the bulk of the food (240 calories per hour of work, compared with 100 calories for big-game hunting) and therefore have equal status with men in many hunter-gatherer societies.

When women hunt, it is commonly for smaller game, while men traditionally hunt the bigger species. In a typical hunter-gatherer society a woman feeds her immediate family, whereas when a man hunts big game, the meat is shared out among the whole group. The clichéd image of man the hunter bringing dinner back to his mate is wrong.

A hunter gains honour and status by killing a big animal and sharing the meat. There are often complicated rules for dividing the carcass. In some societies the hunter traditionally gets the worst

▲ **Modern humans have lived as hunter-gatherers for more than 99 per cent of our history. This lifestyle has inevitably shaped our bodies and minds.**

bits of the kill but receives great prestige for sharing.

This social pressure to give away meat and hides means that younger, stronger people support elderly and sick people. Old people do not need to hunt and instead contribute to the band in other ways, such as by looking after young children, or by acting as repositories of knowledge. A band that looks after its elderly has a wealth of information and experience at its fingertips. This gave *Homo sapiens* a terrific advantage over other predators and earlier forms of hominids.

63

that – along with bone and shell tools – may have been more common in daily use than stone.

There is no direct evidence revealing the kind of wooden tools the first Aborigines possessed, but they almost certainly had the two items common to all hunter-gatherer cultures: the spear and the digging stick (used by women for gathering food and occasionally for fighting). Stone spearheads were not required, perhaps because wooden or bone spearheads were perfectly serviceable for hunting big game. Another weapon common in Australia today is the throwing stick, so we can speculate that the first people had these. True boomerangs were not invented until much later. To carry the food they speared or collected, early Australians almost certainly had dishes made of wood or bark and bags made of plant fibre or animal skin.

A few bone tools have been found. Some are interpreted as fishing lures – when dragged through the water they look like tiny fish. Others have abrasive marks that indicate their use: some were awls and scrapers used to pierce and prepare animal skins; some were spearheads; others

▲ Nineteenth-century Aborigines wearing possum-skin cloaks. The cloaks were worn fur-side inwards and rubbed on the outside with fat to make them waterproof.

were toggles or cloak pins for securing clothing. Having to cope with a cooler climate than that of modern Australia, the first people wore more clothing than Aborigines in historical times did, perhaps making garments like the possum-skin cloaks once worn in Victoria.

Because they had a more sparse and scattered population, Pleistocene Australians may have been more mobile than modern or historical Aborigines. Their lifestyle was geared to making immediate use of any resources that presented themselves as they travelled, rather than gathering food to bring back to a base camp and store for later use.

Cycle of Fire

Australia was a dry land, dominated by fire for millions of years before humans arrived. The consequence is that parts of modern Australia have a 'fire ecology' – the plants are adapted to survive fire and, in fact, often *require* fire to complete their life cycle. These plants have hard, woody seeds and fruits that need to be scorched or burnt to trigger germination. They possess insulating bark thick enough to protect tissues underneath from flames, including new buds that grow beneath the bark. The well-known eucalyptuses have highly flammable oils in their leaves, which create a very intense but short-lived fire, hence saving the woody parts of the tree from destruction. Because of these adaptations, a eucalyptus woodland can quickly rejuvenate after burning, whereas nonadapted plants would be completely destroyed or take many years to regenerate.

Why does this fire ecology exist? The clue is the increasing aridity of Australia. As the continent progressively dried out over thousands of years, fires started by lightning would have spread further and burnt longer. When the first people arrived, they would have found many habitats where fire was a regular seasonal occurrence.

How did the animals respond to fire? Some medium-sized grazing species, like kangaroos and wallabies, prosper from a burning regime, as fire tends to clear out scrubby undergrowth and encourage the growth of fresh grass. Smaller creatures, like lizards and rodents, do less well, as they are not so able to escape the flames. Even if not killed outright, small animals lose the vegetation that normally hides them, making them more vulnerable to predators. In prehistory browsing species like *Diprotodon* and *Palorchestes* were disadvantaged by fire – the woody scrub that they preferred to eat was burnt, and the dense forests were converted into more open grassy woodland.

Under the influence of fire, ancient Australia probably had a dynamic and changing mix of species. When fire struck an area, kangaroos and grasses predominated for many years afterwards. Then, as denser vegetation gradually grew back, the kangaroos migrated elsewhere and the browsers returned. If large plant-eaters tore apart or pushed over trees as part of their feeding strategy – as African elephants do today – the browsers themselves would have been part of the cycle of change: from woodland scrub to open country with sparse trees, then back to woodland scrub again. So, when humans arrived, how did they fit into this cycle of fire?

GIANT SHORT-FACED KANGAROO

This species (*Procoptodon goliah*) was the bulldog of the kangaroo world, being much more robustly built than modern roos – hence the 'giant' name. The skull was short and deep, providing increased chewing force in the jaw muscles. Like the modern red kangaroo, it stood about 2 m (6½ feet) tall and was about 3 m (10 feet) from nose to tail.

The red kangaroo is the best model for how the giant short-faced kangaroo moved and behaved. Like the red kangaroo, the short-faced would have held its body horizontal to the ground and was adapted for hopping on flat rather than steep or rocky terrain. However, in contrast to living kangaroos, the short-faced kangaroo had only a single toe on its hind feet. Like other extinct kangaroos, such as *Sthenurus*, it may have moved almost exclusively on two legs, making it far more bipedal than modern roos.

The giant short-faced kangaroo's teeth show that it was a browser. It tugged down branches of overhanging acacia, pulled branches off saltbush at about chest height or propped itself up on its tiptoes and tail in order to reach treats higher up in trees.

DEMON DUCK

The 'demon duck' (*Genyornis newtoni*) is a member of a group of large, flightless birds called Dromornithids or *mihirungs* (named after the mythological giant emu of the Tjapwurong Aborigines: the *mihirung paringmal*). Because they are closely related to ducks and geese, *Genyornis* and its relatives have been nicknamed the 'demon ducks of doom'.

At 2.2 m (7 feet), *Genyornis* was about as tall as a male ostrich, but twice the weight (200–250 kg; 441–551 lb). Being so heavily built, it was not a fast mover. The wings were tiny and useless for flight, but *Genyornis* might have flapped them as a display to rivals or mates.

Among its distinguishing features were an enormous beak and huge jaw muscles. The beak and skull structure resembled the nut-cracking beaks of seed- and fruit-eating birds such as parrots. *Genyornis* was a vegetarian, browsing in the higher branches of trees and shrubs like a giraffe. Lacking teeth, it had to swallow stones to help grind up the food in its gizzard. Some palaeontologists suggest that *Genyornis* may even have supplemented its diet by scavenging carcasses or grabbing small prey.

▼ Like the much smaller cassowaries and emus, *Genyornis* may have been aggressive and dangerous if you got too close to its nest.

The Burning Times

Natural fires tend to be seasonal, but humans can light fires wherever and whenever they want. To Aboriginal peoples, fire is not just for keeping warm or cooking meals – bushfires are an important and valuable tool to help manage the land.

But why set fire to the place where you live? In a variety of cultures around the world, bushfires are used to 'make grass'. It is easier for a hunter-gatherer to make a living in an open landscape than in a thick forest. Fire is a quick way of turning forest into more open country. Burning off scrub and undergrowth encourages the growth of new grass shoots and tempts grazing animals into the area. People gain other advantages from starting bushfires: they clear the ground for walking, they improve visibility, provide defence from predators, and they can even be used to drive game while hunting.

When the first people arrived in Australia and started lighting fires, they changed the natural fire ecology of the country in three ways. First, fire-adapted communities suffered burning more often; second, fire-adapted communities burnt at different times of year from the natural fire regime; and third, communities that were not fire-adapted began to suffer more regular burning.

The early Australians increased the frequency of bushfires, thus reducing their intensity. Instead of leaving the vegetation to build up over years or decades until the occasional huge blaze consumed it, these pioneers created smaller fires on a more regular basis, preventing larger conflagrations. This caused changes in the vegetation, adding to the changes caused by the drying climate. It is likely that the more frequent fires favoured grassland and fire-resistant woodland at the expense of the less fire-resistant woodland. People had begun to mould the land to suit their own needs.

▶ Prehistoric Australians changed the landscape of their new continent with their use of fire. To what extent did this affect the future of Australia's monsters?

Good Neighbours

One thing is certain about Australia – humanity and the megafauna coexisted for a long, long time. Even if you assume both a late date for human arrival (51,000 years ago) and an early date for the final demise of the megafauna (46,000 years ago), then people and monsters shared the continent for 5,000 years. If you instead prefer to believe that people arrived early (71,000 years ago) and the megafauna survived until as late as 25,000 years ago, then they had a massive 46,000 years together.

Monster Hunters?

For millennia the weapons that prehistoric hunters used to hunt very big game were stone projectile points for spears, and atlatl darts on arrows. Strangely, until about 6,000 years ago, the Aboriginal tool kit did not include such stone points, and Aborigines never had bows and arrows. Does this mean that they did not hunt big game? Or simply that they relied on wood or bone points to make their kills? After all, the Neanderthals in Europe were hunting elephants with wooden spears 125,000 years ago.

Unlike Pleistocene Europe, Australia has no sites with evidence of mass kills of megafauna, and even individual megafauna kill sites are controversial. One viewpoint is that this lack of kills may not be significant – such sites are rare everywhere in the world. Adherents to this view hold that, as there were no stone-tipped points, there is no preserved evidence to find embedded in a slain *Diprotodon* or *Genyornis*, and thus nothing to point the finger at humans as culprits. But what of the lack of butchery marks on the bones? We would expect to find some evidence that humans had cut up a carcass or cooked joints of meat. So far there is remarkably little evidence of butchery or burning on the bones, so no conclusion can be drawn, other than that people and megafauna lived in the same place at the same time.

MARSUPIAL ELEPHANT

Palorchestes azael is known as the marsupial tapir or the marsupial elephant because it had a short trunk akin to a tapir's mobile upper lip or a very small elephant trunk. It was a large, heavy-bodied animal slightly smaller than a modern rhino, with a skeleton surprisingly like a wombat's, but longer-limbed. Unlike tapirs and elephants, the marsupial elephant could most likely stand up on its hind legs.

Although a herbivore, the marsupial elephant was not an animal to annoy – it used its large, strong forearms to tear apart tree trunks. *Palorchestes* was probably the marsupials' answer to the giant ground sloths of the Americas. It ripped items apart with its clawed hands and then used scoop-like incisors to shovel up fruits, tubers, bark and insect grubs.

▼ **The strange creature in this Northern Territory rock painting has been interpreted as a marsupial elephant with a baby beside it.**

It is interesting to note that where bone projectile points do occur in late Pleistocene Australia, they are invariably made of kangaroo or wallaby foot bones. In fact, remains of smaller animals dominate these archaeological sites. So whatever the answer, the first Australians were unlikely to have been megafaunal specialists – they probably killed small game and may have only rarely hunted large animals.

Monster Art

Australia is famed for its Aboriginal art, both prehistoric and modern. Does this vast and beautiful cultural heritage give us any clues about the megafauna? Possibly. More than 60 pictures of the extinct Tasmanian tiger, or marsupial wolf (*Thylacinus cynocephalus*), are known from mainland Australia. This intriguing creature became extinct there about 2,000–3,000 years ago as a result of the introduction of the dingo some 1,000 years earlier. *Thylacinus* survived in Tasmania until 1936, when the last one died in Hobart Zoo. So the mainland paintings give us one definite instance of an extinct creature being recorded in rock art. But 3,000 years ago is relatively recent. What of megafauna that met their demise 25,000–46,000 years ago?

Claims of the depiction of other extinct Australian creatures in prehistoric art are rare. *Genyornis*, *Palorchestes* and the giant echidna *Zaglossus hacketti* are the only species so far named. The giant echidna has living relatives in New Guinea, so we can recognize its portrait even though the Australian species became extinct about 15,000 years ago. Therefore, these paintings date from at least that period.

The giant echidna isn't giant enough to qualify as megafauna – it is only about 1 m (3 feet) long and 30 kg (66 lb) in weight. So what about the real monsters? *Genyornis*, the so-called demon duck, is portrayed by footprints engraved on rocks. The carvings show very large bird tracks alongside similar engravings of emu and bustard prints. As the emu and bustard tracks are very accurate in size compared to a real footprint, the

◀ The Tasmanian tiger was found throughout mainland Australia until the dingo was introduced by Aborigines, about 4,000 years ago.

CUDDIE SPRINGS

Excavations at Cuddie Springs in northern New South Wales have revealed a large collection of megafaunal bones. Ten species are represented, including *Genyornis*, *Diprotodon* and *Megalania*. Numerous stone tools were also found there in 1991, but whether the people who left the tools lived at the same time as the animals is a mystery.

The site has an incredibly complex sequence of sediments, jumbled together over time by mudslides and slumps. As a result, Cuddie Springs' history is a nightmare for geologists and archaeologists to disentangle. Dr Josephine Flood thinks that megafauna survived there until quite a late date (27,000–36,000 years ago). Mike Smith of the National Museum in Canberra holds the opposite view and thinks that old and young material have been mixed together by erosion and mudslides.

▲ People and *Diprotodon* shared a continent for thousands of years. Did humans hunt this monster marsupial?

Some stone tools from Cuddie Springs are said to be stained with bits of blood, tissue and hair from the butchering of animals. There has been speculation that the blood is from *Diprotodon*. However, the preliminary studies have not been published, so the identity of the blood remains unknown.

bigger tracks have been interpreted as belonging to the much larger *Genyornis*. An alternative explanation is that the big tracks represent the footprints of a mythological giant emu or have some other artistic intention that we no longer understand.

In Kakadu National Park in Arnhem Land, Aborigine Nipper Kapirigi and archaeologist George Chaloupka discovered a rock painting of a strange animal with two babies. It has lots of marsupial features (the shape of its tail, for example) and is very hairy. This picture has been interpreted by some palaeontologists as representing *Palorchestes*. Alternatively, of course, the picture could be of a mythical creature with just a superficial resemblance to *Palorchestes*.

The problem with this monster art is the dating. The newest methods have not been calibrated and tested for rock art, so their results are hard to interpret. The oldest reliable dates for Australian rock art go back to about 6,000 years ago. These are paintings done with beeswax, which can be radiocarbon dated. Another helpful insect is the mud wasp, which makes nests of mud and saliva on rock surfaces. Pieces of these nests can be radiocarbon dated to give an age for the wasp saliva – and hence a minimum age for any painting over which the nest is built. The earliest date this technique has given us is a figure of 20,000 years ago for one of the Bradshaw paintings from the Kimberley, but rock-art experts such as Chris Chippendale of the University of Cambridge believe that Australian art is a lot younger than this, the most venerable examples being a mere 15,000 years old.

A date of only 15,000–20,000 years ago for the demise of the megafauna is very controversial. So what is the answer? Is the art older than we think? Did the megafauna survive longer than was thought? Or are these portraits not prehistoric creatures at all, but mythical beings? If rock art in Australia did not develop until after most of the megafauna were extinct, it could explain why there are few monster paintings.

CLAW GRAFFITI

Many caves in South Australia bear the claw marks of animals scratched into their walls. At Robertson Cave at Naracoorte, the culprit was identified as the marsupial lion, *Thylacoleo*. In some caves in the Mount Gambier region, the megafaunal claw marks have an important difference: instead of being incised on bare walls, here the claw marks are gouged over the top of Aboriginal engravings. Human fingers made patterns in the clay on the walls, and a large, clawed animal evidently used the surface as a scratching post some time later.

MONSTER MYTHS

Bunyip: A feared mythical creature from the Victoria area, the bunyip frequented waterways, killing and eating anyone it caught. It is found in different guises in different stories – a giant, bearded snake, a bird-headed man or a big, four-legged animal with clawed hands. The bunyip has been linked with several extinct animals, including *Megalania*, *Palorchestes* and *Diprotodon*.

Giant emu: The enormous *Genyornis* may have inspired the Tjapwurong Aboriginal legend of the *mihirung paringmal*, or giant emu.

Giant roos: The giant short-faced kangaroo (*Procoptodon*) is alleged to be the source of a story about a war between Aborigines of New South Wales and giant kangaroos. The kangaroos were defeated with fire.

Yamuti: The yamuti are huge animals, rather like giant kangaroos or giant wombats, that once roamed the country of the Adnyamathanha people in South Australia. Only shamans could see the yamuti. It has been suggested that these tales relate to *Procoptodon* or *Diprotodon*.

▼ **An Aboriginal rock painting in the X-ray style, which first appeared over 6,000 years ago and continues to be used today.**

Myths and Monsters

Intriguing but controversial evidence that people hunted the megafauna is found in Aboriginal stories of the Dreaming. All cultures have legends and stories of monsters and fabulous beasts, and Aboriginal societies are no different – but are these stories literal accounts of the time when the first Australians shared their lands with the now extinct megafauna?

These tantalizing interpretations must be approached with care. The Dreaming stories of Aboriginal peoples – as well as their art – are part of the social mechanisms that give their communities a group identity and a sense of belonging to their land and its features. Each story may have a very specific purpose and a very specific body of knowledge to impart, as well as a very specific subset of people to whom it is appropriate to give that knowledge. While these legends could be accounts of the time when early Australians shared their lands with megafauna, interpreting them as Chinese whispers from the Pleistocene is speculative at best.

The End of the Monsters

Towards the end of the Pleistocene, 55 species of animals became extinct in Australia, of which about 39 were megafauna. The rest – such as *Warenja* (a primitive wombat) and the prehistoric cousin of the tiny pilot bird – were smaller. Some species became locally extinct but were not completely wiped out. The koala and wombats, for instance, vanished from western Australia but still thrive in the east.

Few megafaunal species came through this period unscathed. At 90 kg (198 lb) for a big male, the red kangaroo is now the largest of the native Australian mammals. Australia's other megafaunal survivors are the grey kangaroo, antilopine kangaroo, euro, saltwater crocodile, freshwater crocodile, emu and cassowary.

After the extinctions, the continent had no large browsing animals, nor any large terrestrial carnivores. The title of largest marsupial predator fell to the marsupial wolf, which was about the size of a German

▲ Saltwater crocodiles (*Crocodylus porosus*) and freshwater crocodiles (*Crocodylus johnsoni*) are the only reptilian monsters left in Australia since the demise of *Megalania*.

◀ Weighing in at 30–55 kg (66–121 lb), the emu (*Dromaius novaehollandiae*) is one of Australia's few surviving megafaunal animals, but is scrawny compared to the extinct *Genyornis*.

shepherd dog. Australia was no longer a land of lumbering giants – being small or fast was now the key to survival.

There is controversy over the timing of the final extinction of Australia's megafauna. There is substantial evidence to indicate that they survived until about 25,000–30,000 years ago, possibly even a little later – a 22,000-year-old jaw from the prehistoric kangaroo *Sthenurus* was found in Clogg's Cave, Victoria. Some scientists believe that the dates for the final extinction cluster around 46,000 years ago, and that younger dates should be viewed with mistrust. There have even been a few claims for the survival of *Diprotodon* until as late as 6,000 years ago at Lime Springs in New South Wales, but the finds were later shown to be ancient bone fragments mixed with younger charcoal, thus producing a more recent date.

WHODUNIT?

Did humans accelerate the demise of the megafauna in Australia? As the minimum suggested overlap for Aborigines and megafauna is 5,000 years, we can tell that a North-American-style blitzkrieg did not take place in Australia. However, proving or disproving overkill is a difficult matter and will require scrupulous study of megafauna bones and human artefacts for signs that the first Australians hunted giant animals. What we do know is that people deliberately started fires. There may not have been an intent to harm the megafauna, but the effects of human-caused fires may have contributed to the extinction of Australia's monsters.

▶ **Ancestors of modern Aborigines invented 'firestick farming' – a sophisticated form of land management based on the use of fire.**

The Straw that Broke *Diprotodon's* Back

For every scientist that points the finger of blame at humanity for the megafauna's disappearance, there is another who blames the climate. If the megafauna did survive until 25,000 years ago, that date has significance for another reason – it was the start of a climatic downturn that led to the coldest, harshest period of the Ice age. Across Australia large lakes began to dry up, and many completely disappeared by the peak of the Ice age 18,000 years ago.

Perhaps this accelerated drying-out of Australia was the final nail in the megafauna's coffin. Water is ephemeral in the outback and controls the lives of Australia's animals. What if the large browsers like *Diprotodon* and *Procoptodon* had to drink every day? Unable to travel far from water, they faced disaster if the lakes disappeared. Their smaller competitors, such as the red kangaroo, may have survived on foliage alone without needing to drink at all.

Some experts believe that the increasingly arid climate squeezed the megafauna into small groups, isolated from each other by great distances. During times of food shortage, one or other of these small populations might perish. Eventually, after enough of these small local extinctions, the whole species would pass the point of no return.

There also turns out to be a surprising link between ice ages and fire. Burning has a bigger impact on Australia during the intervals (which occur every 30,000 years) when regular El Niño events occur. The impact is larger still if El Niño activity coincides with a cold glacial phase. So, over time, we would expect to see the effect of fires on Australian ecology waxing and waning as El Niño intervals and cold, dry glacial stages moved in and out of phase with each other. The browsing megafauna had times of crisis and times of plenty as they lived through these changes. Into this ecological dance came humanity.

The first Australians may have begun starting fires the moment they set foot on the continent, but their actions initially did not have a big impression on the environment. However, when the next active El Niño interval arose (45,000–35,000 years ago), humans and climate could

▲ Two predators confront each other in ancient Australia. Competition with humans and a changing climate may have driven the giant lizard *Megalania* to extinction.

FARMERS IN ALL BUT NAME

Many traditional Aboriginal societies more closely resemble agricultural societies than 'typical' hunter-gatherer groups, such as the !Kung of the Kalahari. Such Aborigines lead a relatively sedentary life and have intensive land-management practices. They have a social hierarchy based on age and gender; polygamous marriage; and elaborate exchange systems. As such, the lifestyle of modern or historically recorded Aborigines might not be the best models for the society or behaviour of the first Australians.

A series of cultural changes occurred in Australia in the past 3,000–8,000 years, resulting in the Aboriginal societies that we see today. The pattern of languages altered, new styles of art arose, and, about 7,000 years ago, a tool called the spear thrower appeared. Perhaps new waves of migrants brought new customs to Australia or catalysed a change in local traditions. Whatever the cause, by the time Europeans arrived the Aborigines possessed highly complex societies and a sophisticated pattern of land management, based around their use of fire.

unintentionally act together to create a huge impact. From about 40,000 years ago there are clear signs that Aboriginal burning was modifying the character of Australia. Human influence on the environment was greatest in the northeast, where even today El Niño has the biggest effect. Humans' greatest tool – fire – had become a crucial factor in determining Australia's future.

By coincidence the plants that are best adapted to surviving a regular regime of fire are also the least palatable to herbivores. Many, like eucalyptus, contain toxins in their foliage. It is well known that the koala is specially adapted to digest eucalyptus leaves, eating over 1 kg (2¼ lb) a day. But even this tough little beast has to avoid consuming certain types during particular seasons, or it will be poisoned by its food. Perhaps the spread of these inedible plants spelled the downfall of browsers like *Diprotodon* and *Palorchestes*, as they had to travel ever farther in search of sufficient quantities of edible vegetation. Species like the red kangaroo, which can travel great distances to find good grazing, won out over short-range travellers like *Diprotodon*. The conflicting needs to stay close to water but to travel widely in search of food could have pushed the megabrowsers towards an inevitable demise.

So could the true scenario for megafaunal loss be that human fires accelerated an ecosystem disruption already started by natural burning? The first Australians' mastery of fire and knowledge of controlled burning gave them a power not previously possessed by humanity: the ability to modify their environment to suit themselves. Deliberately ignited bushfires were the world's first land-management scheme. The unfortunate side effect of this burning was that the large browsers – and the predators that depended on them – were wiped out.

Pleistocene explorers had discovered a new home, conquered the continent, and shaped the very landscape to their own needs. Australia had changed forever.

▶ **The first Australians may have explored every corner of their continent in a mere 1,000 to 3,000 years after landfall. Eventually, the monsters they discovered disappeared.**

Serengeti of the Ice

Today we are living in paradise. For the past 10,000 years Earth has had a mild and stable climate – but such has not always been the case. Over the previous few hundred thousand years Europe was a place of rapid and dramatic shifts from searing cold to balmy warmth. Sometimes these extreme climate changes took place in less than a generation. Just over 40,000 years ago *Homo sapiens* advanced into this unpredictable northern land, and we made it our own.

▲ When the Ice-age climate was at its harshest, most of Europe was too cold and dry for trees to grow. Tundra and tundra–steppe habitats dominated the landscape.

The Ice-age climate rendered vast tracts of Europe too cold and dry to permit trees to grow. In place of forests were grasslands and tundra. Plants from these two habitats met, mixed and eventually covered much of eastern, central and western Europe. This unique 'tundra–steppe' ecosystem thrived as the Ice-age glaciers advanced, and perished as they thawed.

The tundra–steppe was an immensely rich environment. Although the winters were harsh, the summers were not much cooler than they are today. Unlike the tundra regions of today's Arctic – with their short summer and restricted growing season – Ice-age Europe experienced the same long summers that European latitudes do now. Spring and summer boasted plentiful sunlight and warmth, which encouraged plant growth. The lush grasses, herbs and mosses in turn supported vast herds of grazing animals. Europe and central Asia were indeed the Serengeti of the Ice age.

WINTER WORLD

The time when modern humans first lived in Europe is known to archaeologists as the Upper Palaeolithic. It was not one long, drawn-out ice age, but a series of cold and warm phases. *Homo sapiens* had been living on the frontiers of Europe for 50,000 years, but this changing climate had prevented people from colonizing the continent.

When Europe was in the grip of one of the intensely cold periods, the northern polar ice sheets expanded massively to cover Sweden and Norway. Glaciers also poured outwards from mountainous areas, such as the Alps and the highlands of Scotland, and the snowline was 1,000 m (3,280 feet) below its present level. Winter temperatures dropped as low as –27°C (–17°F) in the north (Denmark) and –20°C (–4°F) in France. In the savage winters of the glacial maximum – the time when the climate reached its most extreme – there may have been further drops of another 20–25°C (36–44°F). At the peak of

the Ice age even the warmest summer month would reach only 10–11°C (50–52°F) – equivalent to that of today's Arctic tundra.

In addition to freezing temperatures, it was dry: rainfall and snowfall were roughly half that of today. Most rain fell in the summer months. Surprisingly, it was also dusty. The grinding action of glaciers and the lack of forest exposed northern soils to erosion. Fierce winds picked up the dirt and hurled it southwards. The fertile farmland of central Europe today is actually a thick layer of this windblown soil (loess) – the heritage of Ice-age dust storms.

It was during one of the cold, dry periods, 41,000–39,000 years ago, that *Homo sapiens* pioneers first explored Europe. A second, more severe cold period (the glacial maximum) started around 25,000 years ago and lasted until 13,000 years ago. During this latter time, conditions in the northern reaches of Europe – places like Britain – became so

Just as tundra and grassland plants came together to form the tundra–steppe vegetation, so animals from both north and south invaded this bountiful new environment. For the first time Arctic creatures like muskoxen, reindeer and wolves mingled with such African species as lions and spotted hyenas. The result was an incredibly diverse assembly of animals, dominated by large herds of megafaunal herbivores, which carnivores hunted in packs. *Homo sapiens* was another pack-living predator added to the mix.

harsh that many animals could not survive and were driven out.

There were also warmer times within the Ice age – not true interglacials like today's climate, but brief reigns of milder conditions. Following in the wake of the warmer weather, trees spread back into Europe. Deciduous woodland covered the south, and more hardy coniferous trees reached central Europe. Tundra–steppe continued to hold sway in the north and expanded again after each warm interval was over. At 39,000 years ago there was a rapid shift to one of these warmer climates, lasting some 3,000 years. It was during this relatively mild period of the Ice age that *Homo sapiens* consolidated its foothold in Europe.

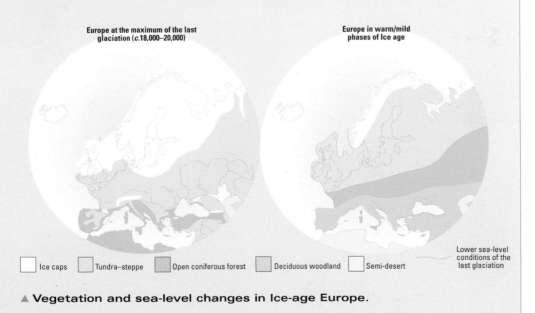

Europe at the maximum of the last glaciation (c.18,000–20,000)

Europe in warm/mild phases of Ice age

| | Ice caps | | Tundra–steppe | | Open coniferous forest | | Deciduous woodland | | Semi-desert |

Lower sea-level conditions of the last glaciation

▲ **Vegetation and sea-level changes in Ice-age Europe.**

The Discovery of Europe

People were not an unusual sight in Europe 40,000 years ago. Small bands of hunter-gatherers had been there for 300,000 years, expanding and contracting their geographical range as the climate waxed and waned. These first people were not modern humans, but were instead offshoots of the archaic *Homo sapiens*. With short, stocky physiques and broad, flat noses, they were extremely well adapted to the cold. We know them as the Neanderthals (*Homo neanderthalensis*).

For more than 250,000 years the Neanderthals had Europe to themselves. Then, in the space of 4,000 or 5,000 years, a new type of humanity entered Europe from the Near East and spread across the continent. Europe now had two human species living side by side; *Homo sapiens* had arrived.

Fully modern people had been in the Near East since about 100,000 years ago and had successfully travelled eastwards across India and Southeast Asia. Yet, for almost 50,000 years, they stalled at the gates of Europe. An indefinable something prevented them entering. That something may have been the climate. Prehistoric *Homo sapiens* – although heavily built compared to present-day people – had a slender, long-limbed body typical of warmer climes. This made these modern humans less suited to the cold winters of Palaeolithic Europe.

Without a stocky Neanderthal physique, *Homo sapiens* was locked out of the cold north. A few brave families may have ventured in now and again, but only as fleeting visitors until a revolution occurred: technological and cultural change.

The technology that enabled us to move north was a simple but profound one: sewing. Simple stitching of hides had probably been around for some time, but now came the innovation of tailored clothes. Instead of a simple cloak draped across the shoulders or kilt wrapped around the waist, these new people manufactured form-fitting clothes. Garments like trousers, leggings, tunics, parkas, hoods, moccasins, boots and mittens would all have been vital in conquering the tundra–steppe. Neatly stitched double seams would keep out the wind. Clothing could

▶ **One of the great inventions of the Ice age: bone needles helped mankind to conquer the harsh climates of northern Europe and Asia.**

be layered, with heavy outer garments and lighter inner ones. Furs could be worn hair-side in for warmth, or hair-side out to take advantage of a particular fur's water-repellent properties.

Sewing is not just about making clothes. Tents of animal skins were also manufactured, again with a view to rendering them windproof and waterproof. This need for particular types of hide brought about a new way of hunting: instead of opportunistically catching whatever they encountered, as the Neanderthals probably did, modern people deliberately set out to seize particular species for their skins.

Deliberate hunting of specific prey is demonstrated by a second technological innovation: special weapons and tactics. The Neanderthal tool kit was a generic one, with a basic spear serving to kill all sorts of medium to large animals. *Homo sapiens* instead produced a whole range of different tools in different materials – stone, wood, bone and antler – each suited to hunting certain animals in particular ways. A large and heavy blade suitable for penetrating mammoth hide is not the right tool to tackle smaller prey like reindeer, or to use as a fishing spear; nets were used for rabbits rather than bison. Upper-Palaeolithic hunters decided in advance what kind of animals to hunt and then took the appropriate weapons with them.

Some of the cultural changes that enabled modern humans to thrive in Europe, and later in central Asia, are already present in the Australian story: the tradition of sharing that makes a hunter-gatherer group function as a community rather than as a loose collection of individuals is the cornerstone of survival. The first fully modern humans appear to have hit upon the idea of extending their community beyond that of the immediate group. In the same way that people living in Orkney and Cornwall all think of themselves as British, widely scattered groups of *Homo sapiens* across Europe may have thought of themselves as 'Aurignacian'.

Today people proclaim their group affiliations with badges, clothing, flags and hairstyles, among other things. The actual items are different, but we have evidence that prehistoric *Homo sapiens* had similar ways of establishing tribal identity. Some of the tools were deliberately made in a particular style, as if to fit a pattern, not a function. These people had long-distance trade (items like seashells were moved 700 km, or 435 miles) and distinctive art imagery, such as 'goddess' figurines that spanned a huge geographical range. The implication is that groups had much social contact, involving trade, intermarriage and the sharing of news about distant people and areas. The Aurignacians most likely helped each other out in times of crisis, donating stored food, pooling resources, or temporarily moving into another group's hunting grounds. Acts like this may not have been conceivable for the less socially adept Neanderthals. To a Neanderthal, any group of strangers may have appeared to be competitors. But to *Homo sapiens*, the fact that the strangers wore a particular style of clothing, carried a certain type of spear point, or had distinctive body decoration, enabled them to be identified as potential allies, even if you did not know them personally.

The tools that enabled these people to make the move into the tundra–steppe were their awls and needles. The tools that enabled them to thrive were their weapons and their minds.

Human Monsters Meet

One intriguing question about the occupation of Europe by our species is: how did we interact with the Neanderthals? Was there coexistence or conflict? The arrival of a new species with similar habits and lifestyle would inevitably lead to competition for living space and resources. But was there open aggression or just a gradual squeezing out of the Neanderthals as they declined and our numbers grew? Certainly there was peaceful contact in some areas, as the Neanderthals learned some of the moderns' tool-making techniques and attempted to mimic our jewellery.

THE AURIGNACIANS

Exactly when did modern humans arrive in Europe? The oldest direct evidence comes from burial sites 32,000–33,000 years old. However, other evidence suggests an earlier arrival. The clues are distinctive types of stone, bone and ivory tools that made a sudden appearance in Europe, marking the arrival of what archaeologists call the Aurignacian culture.

Precursors of the Aurignacian tools appeared first in Bacho Kiro in Bulgaria 43,000 years ago and then in southwest Europe 39,000 years ago. The apparently rapid east-to-west spread makes it difficult to work out what route was taken by the people who fashioned these tools. Most likely, the Bacho Kiro tool makers were the pioneers, entering Europe from the east, either via Greece and the Balkans, or possibly by going around the Black Sea and across the Ukraine. Another suggestion is that proto-Aurignacian pioneers also came from North Africa via Gibraltar to give us the southwestern tools, before

▶ **A carved Aurignacian pendant.**

moving east – but this western route has fewer supporters. Regardless of the route, modern *Homo sapiens* was in Europe by about 40,000 years ago.

As long-time inhabitants of the subtropics, the pioneers would have been black-skinned and physically very different from the stocky Neanderthals. But it was their cultural, not physical, differences that enabled the Aurignacians to displace the Neanderthals and conquer a continent. They were the first true Europeans.

Trees, not people, may have been the Neanderthals' nemesis. They were not a forest species – when trees advanced, Neanderthals retreated, as they found it harder to survive in the warm woodland environments. It may be no coincidence that the Aurignacian pioneers consolidated their hold on Europe when the climate was milder and tree cover had spread as far north as France and southern Poland. By 34,000 years ago

CAVE BEAR

One of the true monsters of the Ice age was the cave bear (*Ursus spelaeus*). It was one of the world's biggest bears, coming close to an Alaskan grizzly (*Ursus arctos*) in size. The cave bear is estimated to have weighed between 400 and 700 kg (882–1,544 lb), with the males almost twice the weight of females. For comparison, adult European brown bears are usually only 95–390 kg (209–860 lb). The cave bear was most numerous in western Europe, although its remains have been found as far east as the Caspian Sea.

The cave bear had a stout body and a large head with massive canine teeth. Cave paintings show it as having short ears and a pig-like face – making it look like a giant, if dangerous, teddy bear. Despite the cave bear's large size, its teeth show us that it was largely vegetarian – even more so than living brown bears. It probably specialized in digging up roots from the deep silt left by glaciers, as modern grizzlies do. The cave bear may have included a little meat in its diet by digging up burrowing animals such as marmots, and by catching spawning salmon and sturgeon.

The bear gets its name from the thousands of its bones found in caves. Cave bears hibernated in caves and probably gave birth there. Their footprints have been found on cave floors, their claw marks are on the walls, and in narrow passages their fur has

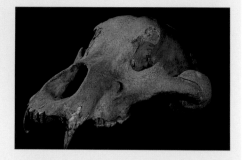

▲ Skull of a cave bear. Despite its large canine teeth, the cave bear had a vegetarian diet. The canines may have been to threaten rivals away from food.

even polished the rock smooth. One cave in Austria contained the remains of 30,000–50,000 bears, indicating that it had been in use for many generations.

A good cave for a bear to hibernate in would also be a good cave for humans to use as shelter or for painting. People, cave bears and brown bears all sought the same caves, but not necessarily at the same time. Disputes over ownership would have been dangerous, so people may have wisely avoided caves when they knew bears were in residence.

The cave bear's fate may have been linked to that of its competitor, the brown bear – as one species thrived, the other declined. Brown bears pushed cave bears out of Britain 100,000 years ago. Elsewhere in Europe, the cave bear fared better – until the ice retreated, and the cave bear grew increasingly rare until it finally became extinct.

Aurignacian stone tools are found all across Europe, but Neanderthal tools were by then confined to small regions. By the time the climate switched back to one that favoured the Neanderthals, their former lands were occupied by *Homo sapiens*. The Neanderthals no longer had any space to expand into. About 30,000 years ago the last of these human monsters became extinct.

A Palaeolithic Bestiary

Many of Europe's megafaunal mammals are familiar to us today: red deer, reindeer, bison, brown bears, wolves. Some, like the cave lion and cave hyena, were really modern species in an Ice-age guise, heftier variants of the African lion and the spotted hyena, their increased body size being an adaptation to life in cold climates. Other European monsters, such as aurochs (wild cattle), giant deer (or Irish elk), cave bears, woolly rhino and woolly mammoth are now extinct.

The types of megafauna to be found varied with the climate. In warmer phases of the Ice age, forest-loving animals colonized Europe along with the advancing treeline. Fallow deer, wild boars, aurochs and leopards became more common. Animals that favoured warmer conditions – like the straight-tusked elephant and hippopotamus – also thrived. When the climate was colder and grasslands or tundra prevailed, reindeer, wild horses, bison, lions, woolly rhino and woolly mammoth were dominant. Reindeer and bison increased in abundance as woolly rhino and mammoth decreased, probably because the latter are not as well adapted to the harshest conditions. In fact, when the Ice age was at its height, some large mammals – including woolly rhino and humans – seem to have been driven out of northern Europe altogether, abandoning Britain and Germany.

As well as bones and footprints, Palaeolithic Europe has one additional and magnificent source of information about the megafauna – prehistoric art. Carvings, engravings and paintings of animals are found all across central and southern Europe, with France and Spain the main centres of

WOOLLY RHINOCEROS

The woolly rhino (*Coelodonta antiquitatis*) entered Europe at least 170,000 years ago, so it was a long-term resident of the continent by the time modern humans appeared. It occupied all of Europe except ice-bound Scandinavia and the warmer regions of southern Italy and southern Greece. The woolly rhino was a grazing animal, similar in habits to the modern white rhino (*Ceratotherium simum*), but was superbly adapted to the colder climates of temperate and tundra–steppe grasslands.

▲ **Woolly rhino weighed almost 2 tons, and were thus invulnerable to most predators.**

How do we know that the woolly rhino *was* woolly? By good fortune a number of frozen carcasses, complete with long, shaggy fur, have been found in Siberia. There is even a pickled rhino from a salt deposit in Spain. These rhino remains provided a surprise in the shape of the horn, which is a flattened sword shape rather than the usual cone. Each horn is worn away on the underside, indicating that the woolly rhino used its horn to sweep away winter snow in order to uncover grass.

Many images of woolly rhinos were painted at Chauvet Cave alongside lions, bears and horses. Did the people who painted these pictures do so out of respect for an animal as dangerous as a lion or cave bear? Or did they hunt it?

this art world. The oldest art was created very soon after human arrival. Images of rhinos at Chauvet Cave were painted 32,400 years ago, while ivory carvings from Hohlenstein-Stadel in southwest Germany are 32,000 years old. Carnivores like bears and lions predominate in the earliest art, while herbivores were the preferred subjects later on.

Prehistoric artists painted and carved animals for very specific reasons – their art is not just random creative expression. They never, for example, painted landscapes or the sky, and images of insects or plants are rare. The majority of the pictures are of cryptic symbols or large

▲ Many cave paintings of aurochs (*Bos primigenius*) were painted life-size – some 2 m (6½ feet) high at the shoulder.

plant-eating mammals, with carnivorous mammals, people, fish and birds being less common subjects. Some small animals – like rodents – are not painted or carved at all, even though we know that they shared caves and campsites with the artists.

Horses win first prize for being the most painted animals, with bison coming a close second and aurochs in third place. One would imagine that the choice of topic reflected what people were hunting, but this is not the case. Hunters of southwest Europe, where the bulk of the art occurs, preferred to kill reindeer and red deer. Horses, bison and aurochs were hunted on a much smaller scale. It is likely that the art had a religious or social function, possibly related to our need to create a strong sense of tribal identity.

Prehistoric art gives us information that we could not get from animal bones alone. Paintings tell us that the extinct European steppe bison (*Bison priscus*) was closer in appearance to the European forest bison (*Bison bonasus*) than to the American plains bison (*Bison bison*), for instance. Steppe bison did not have the thick woolly hair on the head that gives the American bison its typical 'bonnet', so their horns appear more prominent in the paintings. Nor did they have such a long beard or such woolly forelegs. The steppe bison may have been a paler colour than the forest bison, if the pigments chosen by the prehistoric artists were an accurate reflection of its coat.

From paintings at Chauvet Cave, we also know that the male European lion had little or no mane. These lions had only the sparse manes of adolescents rather than the luxuriant manes of adults.

▲ **Wild horses are the most frequently painted animals in European Ice-age art. The quality** of painting prompted Picasso to remark of contemporary art, 'we have discovered nothing'.

Prehistoric art can also tell us about travel and trade. Beautiful engravings of seals have been found 450 km (280 miles) from the nearest Upper Palaeolithic seashore. These pictures must have been carved by someone who had observed living animals. The carvings were then either traded further inland or carried by the artist when he or she travelled away from the coast, and they remain a prehistoric mystery.

Could some paintings form a map of important features of the landscape and the seasonal movements of animals? Only certain areas of the caves were used to paint animals (although there is ample space elsewhere), and only certain caves were used (although there are other seemingly identical ones nearby). The placement of animal images within caves appears to reflect features of the country outside – a zoological map. If the paintings are interpreted in this way, the locations that received the most attention from the artists were rivers. It seems that the places where and times when animals crossed rivers were of great importance to Palaeolithic people, possibly because the hunting was easier.

▲ The European lion was a northern variant of the African and Asian lion. It is also known as the cave lion, because its bones are often found in British caves.

Life, Death and Art

It would be wrong to think of the Upper-Palaeolithic Europeans as a homogenous, continent-wide society that existed unchanged for 30,000 years. These people were culturally diverse across time, with differing funeral rites and hunting practices, and a continuing evolution in the style and range of their tools and art. At any one time, however, there were similarities between widely separated groups, as well as trade and ceremonial gatherings. People of the Eurasian steppes lived in small and nomadic bands during the Ice age, which helped to promote cultural stability; people did not settle down and develop an isolated, insular village lifestyle with identifiable local traditions until much later.

There are two main sources of information about Palaeolithic culture: art and burials. One widespread tradition was the use of 'Venus' or 'goddess' figurines, found from France to the Ukraine. They are mostly from later cultures, although a few may be as much as 30,000 years old (Aurignacian). More than two hundred of these female figures have been found. They were carved from ivory, stone and amber, or sculpted from clay. Most were hidden in secret places like storage pits or the darkest recesses of caves, and many were deliberately broken, as if the figurine had been ceremonially killed. Both these facts lend credence to the idea that they had religious significance. The clay Venuses of Dolni Vestonice in the Czech Republic met a particularly spectacular 'death' – their makers discovered that the clay would fracture and explode if placed in a hearth or kiln.

The Magdalenian (17,000–11,000 years ago) is known as the 'high art' period of Palaeolithic Europe because most cave art, engravings and carvings date to this time. Magdalenian artists painted the famous caves of Lascaux in France and Altamira in Spain. When Pablo Picasso visited Lascaux in 1940, he compared the images to those of modern art, saying of contemporary artists, 'we have discovered nothing'.

Cave art is mainly found in the southwest of Europe: France and Spain. Strangely, there are no instances of art from Britain, despite suitable caves

▲ Three examples of Venus figures. Nearly all the carved human figurines from Palaeolithic Europe are of women.

being abundant. Perhaps the small fraction of England and Wales not buried in ice had too sparse a population for cave painting to be common or practical. Or it could be that those ancient inhabitants of Britain celebrated their lives and their religion in other ways, for example, dance or song. The oldest known musical instruments in Europe are flutes some 36,800 years old.

Burials are another useful source of information because they show what people deemed important enough to place in the grave with the deceased, and they prove that prehistoric humans believed in an afterlife. There are very few burials known from the early Aurignacian period, although Neanderthal graves date from this time. It may be that the first modern humans in Europe were disposing of their dead by cremating them or exposing them to the elements. In contrast, there are elaborate graves from the later Palaeolithic, such as the multiple burials at Dolni Vestonice. Here some 34 individuals, ranging from isolated bones to complete skeletons, have been found in the world's first cemetery: an outdoor site used repeatedly.

Because Britain was rendered uninhabitable for long periods by the climate, there are few burials to be found there. The best known is the Red Lady of Paviland Cave in south Wales – although the 'lady' in question is actually a young man. At his funeral a mammoth skull was placed over his body. His bones were stained with red ochre, so he was probably wearing clothing that had been coloured red with this pigment. He was also wearing an apron-like garment with periwinkle shells sewn all over it. Placed in the grave with him were several hundred ivory rods with red ochre polished into them to give a red metallic sheen. Such rods

BAUBLES, BANGLES AND BEADS

The inhabitants of Palaeolithic Europe loved jewellery. They made bracelets of ivory and pendants of bone. They strung necklaces from fish vertebrae, arctic fox teeth, deer teeth, seashells and mammoth ivory beads. In fact, 'bead factories' existed – sites where the people dedicated a great deal of time and effort to manufacturing hundreds of ivory or soapstone beads.

People buried their dead in clothing decorated with beads, shells and carved pieces of bone. It is estimated that 3,000 hours of work went into making the beads on the body of one man from Sungir in Russia. Whether people wore this fancy clothing in everyday life we don't know, but it seems likely that they celebrated tribal identity, individuality and status with jewellery, much as we do today.

Some Palaeolithic people may have had tattoos. Very fine, sharp bone needles found at Le Mas d'Azil in France may have been for tattooing. The needles date from the Azilian culture at the very end of the Ice age, some 11,000–9,000 years ago.

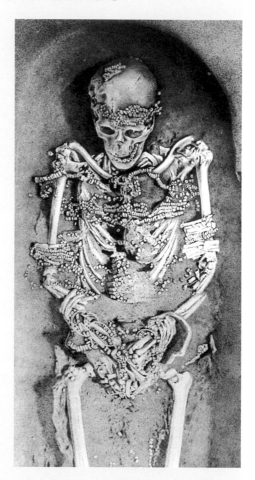

▲ Hundreds of mammoth ivory beads were sewn to the clothing – including a cap – of this man buried at Sungir in Russia about 24,000 years ago.

were probably used for making beads – a section of mammoth ivory would be made into a rod of an appropriate size, then cut into sections and drilled to form beads.

Natural Born Killers

Ice-age Europe was the Promised Land. The huge herds of large herbivores and the highly seasonal environment presented a great opportunity for the adaptable and structured societies of *Homo sapiens*. Whereas the Neanderthals took prey in ones and twos as chance dictated, modern humans had the technical and social know-how to go on communal hunts and kill large numbers of animals at one time. But why kill many animals at once? Isn't this a wasteful way to hunt?

To our eyes mass slaughter might seem illogical, but it may actually be an efficient strategy for a hunter-gatherer. When several hunters cooperate, they can take advantage of the huge glut of animals that pass during the annual migration. If you have a method of storing food, such

AUROCHS

The aurochs (*Bos primigenius*), or wild ox, is the ancestor of European breeds of domestic cattle, and it survived long after the Ice age ended. Our modern cattle are pygmies compared to the aurochs, which stood up to 2 m (6½ feet) high at the shoulder. Bull aurochs were much bigger than the cows and had longer horns that pointed forwards rather than sweeping out to the side. Intriguingly, cave paintings show that aurochs bulls were mostly black, some with a saddle patch of a lighter colour, while cows and calves were red. The habitats preferred by aurochs were forests or open scrub, so they were more numerous in Europe during warmer phases of the Ice age, although still present in colder times. Ancient Greek and Roman writers tell us that the aurochs was an aggressive animal: herd members cooperated to use their great size in defending each other from predators, much as African buffalo gang up to ward off lions. Aurochs were more dangerous prey than reindeer or horses.

as freezing or drying meat, then an opportunity to kill much prey in a short space of time is an advantage. Surplus meat is insurance to see you through the lean times. The Neanderthals most likely thawed out animals that perished in winter to provide food in the cold season. The moderns could add an extra twist to this – deliberately killing large numbers of animals, then freezing them by digging into the permafrost or burying them in snow-covered caches.

Another benefit of mass kills is that you catch animals when their fat content is highest. Arctic animals such as reindeer, moose, bison and saiga antelopes feed up during summer and autumn and rely on their fat reserves to survive the winter. Hunter-gatherers preferred fatter animals, as eating too much lean meat is a risky business – humans need fat to help digest protein, and not getting enough fat can lead to protein poisoning. Many examples of apparent waste can be attributed to hunters taking only the fatty parts of the carcass and abandoning the excess meat. Prehistoric reindeer-hunters at Stellmoor in northern Germany butchered the fattest animals but took only the skins of the leaner ones. These practical people then weighted down the unwanted carcasses with stones and threw them in the lake to avoid attracting hyenas and wolves to their camp.

Like fat the skin was another prized part of the animal – hunters needed high-quality hides both for clothing and shelter. In seasonal environments, animal hides have different properties at different times of the year. In autumn and winter the animals of Ice-age Europe had thick hides with coats of dense winter fur. These thicker hides are most useful for making tough, durable leather for tents and footwear. In spring the animals shed their winter coats and their skin became thinner. Newborn animals especially have very thin and soft skin. If you needed a hide to make soft, flexible leather for clothing, spring was the time to go hunting for it.

Prehistoric Europeans were expert big-game hunters. There is a vast array of evidence of their hunts and many communities specialized in taking just one sort of prey. At some French sites 95 to 99 per cent of the animal bones belong to reindeer, while red deer were the preferred target

A-HUNTING WE SHALL GO

Most large predators target the young, the old or the weak, as these usually involve less risk and effort to hunt. When they kill an animal in the prime of its life, it is usually because the individual in question falls into one of two other categories – the careless or the unlucky. Humans are different and actually specialize in hunting animals in their prime. The only other carnivores to do this regularly are lions, and it provides access to prey with lots of nutritionally valuable fat.

Human hunter-gatherers also select prey for purposes other than filling their bellies. A hunter might want a thick hide for making a tent, antlers to make tools, or a specific colour of fur for religious or aesthetic uses. A lot of planning and skill went into

▲ A reconstruction of a simple hut made from a mammoth-tusk framework. The frame would have been covered in animal hides or turf.

human hunting expeditions – for instance, knowing when was the best time of year to hunt a specific animal – so the impact humans have on animal populations is very different from that of other predators.

in other areas. The reindeer hunters brought home bison or horses as a second choice. Butchered bones of ibex, aurochs, saiga antelopes and moose tell us that these animals were also prey. Archaeologists can reconstruct how the animals were killed: the position and angle of flint points embedded in reindeer bones from Stellmoor reveals that the animals were speared from behind as they swam across a lake.

Did these hunters tackle the largest of the European megafauna, such as woolly rhino and mammoth? Some Neanderthal sites contain butchered woolly rhino carcasses, but there is no evidence that *Homo sapiens* hunted this creature. Modern humans painted images of rhinos, so it might be expected that they prized rhinoceros horn as some do today. However, rhino horn decays very quickly when buried – it is made of

GIANT DEER

The giant deer (*Megaloceros giganteus*) is also known as the Irish elk, although it is not an elk at all – it is related to the fallow deer. It ranged across Europe and Asia from Ireland through Siberia to China, as well as being found in North Africa. Like the woolly rhino, it was not found in the very south of Europe.

The name 'giant deer' comes from its hefty size: it weighed approximately 315–454 kg (695–1,000 lb) and was 2.1 m (7 feet) tall at the shoulder. This makes it as tall as a moose, but a little more lightly built. Its alternative name of Irish elk derives from the predominance of its bones in Irish peat bogs. Remains of the giant deer outnumber all other mammalian remains found in Ireland, with over a hundred individuals recovered from Ballybetagh Bog near Dublin alone.

The giant deer is most famed for the size of its antlers. They were broad and flat like a moose's antlers, and, as in most deer, only the stags possessed them. However, the giant deer's antlers put the moose to shame, spanning up to 4.3 m (14 feet) and weighing 45 kg (99 lbs), which is about a seventh of the deer's total weight. Study of these antlers has shown that they were reinforced for fighting. Some forks were positioned to protect the eyes when the giant deer was engaged in a shoving

▲ **The long-legged and fleet-footed giant deer may have been adapted to out-pace long-distance runners like wolves.**

match with a rival. Cave paintings, such as one in the Cave of Cougnac, France, have been identified as depicting the giant deer, because of a distinctive hump on the animal's shoulders – the mass of bone and muscle needed to support the heavy neck and head. Its skeleton suggests that it was a fast endurance runner – the best athlete the deer family has ever produced. With a tireless, long-legged gait like that of the moose, which can reach speeds of 56 km/h (35 miles/h), the giant deer could wear out predators without itself becoming exhausted.

keratin, the same substance as human fingernails – so any rhino-horn objects that prehistoric *Homo sapiens* might have made are long gone. A rhino skeleton with projectile points embedded in it would be required to prove that today's rhino poaching has an Ice-age precedent.

Mammoths, on the other hand, were definitely hunted. Compared to other creatures, however, they seem not to have been on the menu very often, which is not surprising for such large and dangerous animals. Mammoth ivory was widely used for carvings and beads, but there are not many kill sites – and you can make a lot of beads from one 45-kg (100-lb) mammoth tusk. The mammoth was of greatest importance to the peoples of eastern Europe and the Ukraine, where its bones were used to build huts and windbreaks. The bones probably came both from kills and from natural accumulations of skeletons around salt licks. Most of the bones lack butchery marks, so the majority of the mammoths probably died a natural death, their skeletons being collected later.

Palaeolithic people certainly hunted the small European brown bear, but evidence that they hunted cave bears is scarce. A few cave bears were found with what looked like spear damage to the skull, but this was proved to be caused by a degenerative bone disease, not a wound inflicted by a hunter. The cave bear was perhaps too large and dangerous for Ice-age Europeans to hunt.

Homo sapiens did not just hunt big game – small mammals and birds were an important part of the economy too. Brown hares, mountain hares, badgers, grouse, ptarmigans, ducks, geese and swans were all caught for food. Beavers, otters, martens, red foxes and arctic foxes were hunted for their pelts, and birds of prey were also hunted, probably for their feathers. Most of these smaller creatures would have been trapped, snared or netted. People were weaving nets some 29,000–22,000 years ago, as shown by imprints of knotted fibres found in clay from prehistoric settlements in the Czech Republic. Net hunting is a group activity – men, women and children would have participated in driving the animals and a well-organized net hunt could easily supply as much food as a big-game hunt, with the added benefit that there was considerably less risk of injury.

Nasty, Brutish and...er...Long?

Because Europe offers us more human skeletons to study than other regions, we can start to piece together information about the health and longevity of prehistoric people. Their bones have a variety of fractures from accidents – bumps on the head, broken arms, and so on. Perhaps surprisingly, prehistoric Europe seems to have been a peaceful place, because these broken bones show no evidence of being caused by human violence. Hunting accidents were probably responsible for most injuries. Interestingly, they are equally common among men and women, so both sexes must have participated in hunts. Neanderthals suffered the same types of fracture, but far more often than the modern humans did. In a Neanderthal world everyone would have had at least one broken bone by the time they reached the age of 30. In *Homo sapiens* the rate drops dramatically, with perhaps only 10 or 20 per cent of people suffering this type of accident. Modern Europeans were obviously more careful or clever on their hunts – a demonstration, perhaps, of the advantage of long-distance weapons like the atlatl (see Chapter 4).

Careful or not, there was one particular form of broken bone that spelled disaster. Late Palaeolithic burials have yet to reveal anyone with a leg injury severe enough to prevent them walking. This was a nomadic people, and everyone in the band had to be able to travel long distances. Anyone unable to keep up was probably abandoned.

This mobile lifestyle had another drawback. In a few skeletons the hands show signs of arthritis caused by carrying or dragging something. Either the person carried a very heavy load now and again, or they continually used their hands to drag a lighter load. Pulling a travois or a hide loaded with food or possessions could have caused this affliction.

Despite difficulties in accurately ageing skeletons (human ageing is all a matter of wear and tear and genetics), we know that there were greater numbers of elderly people among the early modern humans than among the Neanderthals. Elderly people were almost nonexistent in Neanderthal populations, but were common in *Homo sapiens*. Age had become a resource rather than a handicap.

End of the Ice

Thirteen thousand years ago, the climate of Europe became milder, allowing forests to advance again from the south. But this warm phase was different: it did not end with a return to the cold. Instead, 10,500 years ago, there was an abrupt and dramatic change, leading to the climate we have today. The Ice age was at an end.

Within a mere 25–50 years, England's climate was transformed from an Arctic to a warm temperate. In the wake of this rapid change the forests accelerated their advance and had conquered the north. In response tundra plants retreated northwards, following the cold. The

MAN THE HUNTER, WOMAN THE BUTCHER

The hunting of animals as big as mammoth may have profoundly affected prehistoric society. Traditionally in hunter-gatherer societies, men hunt larger game, while women gather plants and hunt smaller animals. If truly enormous animals were available to hunt, how might this affect the traditional roles of men and women?

On one hand, men could hunt less often, because one enormous kill would provide as much food as several smaller kills. The men would therefore have more free time, allowing them to take more responsibility for childcare, spend more time making tools and other items, or simply while away the hours by socializing and gossiping. On the other hand, men might go hunting just as frequently as before, increasing their overall contribution to the communal food supply. As a result, the women would not need to collect as much food, potentially giving them more free time.

However, in hunter-gatherer groups who, in recent times, obtained enormous amounts of food from mass kills (such as the Greenland Eskimos hunting migrating caribou), the women did not end up with more leisure time at all. Instead, tasks like skinning and butchering the carcasses, preserving the meat, and tanning the hides became almost exclusively women's work.

◄ Ice-age harpoon point from Europe. Both men and women used harpoons to hunt fish.

▲ As the climate warmed up, the spreading forests forced many megafauna to withdraw eastwards and on to the Asian steppes, where some survive today.

steppe grasses, however, could not cope with the short growing season and harsh winters of the Arctic, so they did not migrate as far. Steppe plants and tundra plants were no longer found together: the unique tundra–steppe habitat ceased to exist.

Plants, Climate and Destiny

With the end of the tundra–steppe, the animals that had been so abundant in Ice-age Europe faced an uncertain future. Those that could not cope with warmer conditions were forced to follow the tundra north. The muskox and the woolly mammoth underwent such a range migration and

THE VANISHING

Europe's megafauna did not simply disappear in one fell swoop. Even before the arrival of *Homo sapiens* on the continent, some species were struggling to survive. The first casualties were those animals that had thrived in milder times. The advancing ice forced them to take refuge in the warmest parts of Europe, south of the Alps and Pyrenees.

Straight-tusked elephants, hippopotamus and narrow-nosed rhinos were driven out of more northerly climes about 72,000 years ago, and regions like Iberia became the sites of their last stand. The hippopotamus most likely perished just a few thousand years before modern humans entered Europe. The other species clung on, but when the climate became even colder, they were doomed. The last of the straight-tusked elephants died in Portugal 30,000 years ago, and the narrow-nosed rhino vanished 5,000–10,000 years later.

More extinctions occurred between the peak of the Ice age (18,000 years ago) and its end (10,000 years ago). This time the animals that succumbed were cold-loving species, such as mammoth, steppe bison, European tahr (a type of mountain goat), cave bear and woolly rhino. The giant deer, however, managed to survive past the end of the Ice age – some skeletons found on the Isle of Man are only 9,200 years old. A few animals, such as the spotted hyena, the muskox and the saiga antelope, abandoned Europe but survive elsewhere.

The Taimyr Peninsula in the northernmost reaches of Siberia seems to have been a final refuge for the Pleistocene megafauna. The woolly mammoth survived there until about 10,000 years ago, and wild horses were present until a few thousand years later. Muskoxen bones show that they managed to endure until as late as 2,900 years ago.

suffered the hidden costs of the move. Because the Arctic has less intense sunlight and a shorter summer than have lower latitudes, there is less plant growth. The number of animals that the region can sustain is therefore smaller. As they withdrew north, the huge herds of central and southern Europe dwindled in size. Competition between the survivors would have been intense. Eventually, some species may have been driven to extinction by their rivals.

SIZE DOES MATTER

When the climate is cold, being big is an advantage for mammals. A large animal has a small surface area relative to its weight, so it loses heat proportionally more slowly. Babies, for example, suffer the effects of hypothermia faster than adults. To help withstand the cold, many of Europe's Ice-age animals – lions, hyenas, bears, red deer – were much larger than their modern temperate or tropical counterparts.

But being big has its disadvantages too. For a start, you need more food than a small animal. This is fine when you live in the rich tundra–steppe of central Europe, but what happens when you are forced to migrate to the Arctic tundra as the Ice age ends? There is a dilemma: should you stay large to ward off the cold, or shrink to cope with the poorer pickings? The Eurasian woolly mammoth opted for the latter. As the range of the species contracted and its numbers dwindled, the mammoth became smaller. On Wrangel Island in Siberia – the last stand of the mammoth – a dwarf form existed, only 1.8 m (6 feet) tall. A little over 4,000 years ago the Wrangel Island mammoths finally perished. Perhaps there had finally come a point when the mammoths could not get any smaller without succumbing to the cold.

▼ **Woolly mammoths survived in the Taimyr Peninsula, Siberia, until about 10,000 years ago and for a few thousand years later on Wrangel Island.**

A variant of this fate befell those that followed the cold by travelling not north but up into the mountains. The higher the fauna and flora climbed, the smaller the actual area they had to live in. The cave bear retreated to higher altitudes as glaciers melted, seeking out the colder temperatures and the alpine vegetation it needed to survive. This retreat, coupled with rivalry with brown bears, may have spelled its downfall. By 10,000 years ago the cave bear was extinct.

The animals that depended on the more productive steppes may have had a third destiny – either corralled in Europe's gradually shrinking grasslands until the trees overwhelmed them, or being forced to withdraw eastwards to the Asian steppes. This was the fate of Europe's wild horses. The tarpan inhabited the Ukrainian steppes until the end of the nineteenth century, while Przewalski's horse was pushed to Mongolia.

A fourth strategy may have been open to those animals that could successfully adapt to both a warmer, wetter climate and the forests that accompany this: they could stay put. Aurochs, wolves, brown bears and red deer all made the transition to forest life, having always favoured areas with some woodland. They were joined by animals that advanced north with the trees, such as the roe deer, the European forest bison and the wild boar.

Blood on Their Hands?

Did humans have a hand in any of these extinctions? Some people believe that prehistoric hunters were responsible for megafauna extinctions in Europe. On the face of it this seems unlikely, because the most heavily hunted species – reindeer and red deer – survived the end of the Ice age, while species for which there is little evidence of hunting – such as mammoths and cave bears – did not.

▶ Wolves successfully adapted to the warmer climate and thrived as forest spread into post-Ice-age Europe; they only later became endangered as a result of conflict with farmers.

THE MYTH OF METABOLIC EXTINCTION

A popular misconception is that the giant deer became extinct because of the 'huge metabolic demand' of growing and shedding its antlers every year. This theory postulates that the male giant deer wasted too much energy on its huge antlers and the species as a whole perished when there was not enough food to support the antler-growing habit. It neglects, however, the fact that the females of many large mammals (deer, horses and antelopes, for example) grow and shed and feed a baby every year without facing metabolic ruin. Female reindeer even manage to regrow antlers as well.

If there was not enough food for the giant deer stags to grow their antlers, there was certainly not enough food for the hinds to support a pregnancy or provide milk for their offspring. Lack of babies would be a far quicker route to extinction for the giant deer than loss of antlers. Long before antler growth threatened the health of the largest males, we would expect natural selection to favour females that produced a smaller fawn or shortened pregnancy or the length of time they produced milk. The overall result would then be a reduction in adult deer size, and the antlers should scale down in proportion to the rest of the body.

Did this happen? Shrinking prehistoric deer are seen at the end of the Ice age. The giant deer stags in Ireland at the time of the final extinction were smaller than those of earlier times. At 56–255 kg (123–562 lb), modern British red deer stags are 200–400 kg (441–882 lb) lighter than their Ice-age counterparts. It seems that while the red deer successfully made this transition to a smaller body size, the giant deer attempted it but ultimately failed. Perhaps it was not big antlers but big babies that spelled the downfall of the giant deer.

▲ Reindeer stags start to grow new antlers in spring and shed the sensitive velvet layer in autumn, just before the rut.

▲ Reindeer cross rivers and fjords on their migrations and are vulnerable to ambush by hunters at these locations. During the Ice age they were extensively hunted by humans in Europe.

Humans were probably not the culprits in the case of the giant deer. It was abundant in Ireland towards the end of the Ice age, finally dying out about 10,700 years ago. People did not reach Ireland until 1,600 years after the giant deer was gone, so humanity is unlikely to have been responsible for its disappearance.

Determining cause and effect can be tricky. Computer simulations are one way of trying to guess what might have happened. Professor Stephen Mithen of the University of Reading conducted a mathematical analysis of how mammoths might respond to human hunting. He discovered that mammoth hunting was sustainable if humans killed two per cent or less of the population each year. Mithen suggested that this level of hunting was practised by the peoples of northern Europe and the Ukraine, thus

THE HUNT GOES ON

In contrast to Europe's Ice age, the millennia that followed the melting of the ice caps have thrown up plenty of evidence for human hunters killing off animals. Pygmy forms of the straight-tusked elephant and the hippopotamus had evolved on various Mediterranean islands, such as Cyprus. These animals survived the extinction of their mainland cousins, but perished when humans colonized the islands some 8,000–9,000 years ago. Lions became extinct in western and northern Europe at the end of the Ice age, but we know that they survived in the Balkans and Greece until at least classical times, because the Ancient Greeks wrote about lion hunts. In the face of this hunting, the lion soon vanished from Europe altogether. The aurochs adapted well to forest life but continued to be preyed on by humans. In Britain it had been driven to extinction by the Bronze Age. The last European aurochs was killed in Poland in 1627.

enabling them to continue their lifestyle for thousands of years. Computer simulations of climate change also predict reduced numbers of mammoths, but again not enough to threaten extinction. A series of these climate-related population declines is known from the fossil record.

The crunch comes when climate change and the two per cent rate of hunting are combined: in such instances the mammoths drop to dangerously low numbers. Such a drastically reduced population is very vulnerable to extinction from a whole variety of causes — further climatic upheaval, increased hunting, local disease outbreaks, food shortages and plain bad luck. When an animal population dwindles and splits into small groups it can be wiped out by what are effectively statistical accidents. A single bout of bad weather, for instance, can kill off vulnerable youngsters.

We do not know the hunting rates of the Upper-Palaeolithic Europeans, but the scarcity of butchered mammoth bones hints that it was less than two per cent. We also do not know the exact effect of food shortages and competition with other animals when the mammoth herds moved north on to the less fertile Arctic tundra. But we do know that

▲ Did the disappearance of the tundra–steppe grasslands of Eurasia result in the extinction of megafauna like the woolly rhino? The last woolly rhino died around 12,500 years ago.

some – if not all – of these factors combined lethally to wipe out not only mammoth, but also the woolly rhino, the giant deer, the steppe bison, the European tahr and the cave bear, and to drive others – like the muskox – out of Europe altogether.

New Frontiers

With its complex social organization, versatile way of life and technological innovations, *Homo sapiens* had conquered the open spaces of the Eurasian tundra–steppe. Sometimes there were setbacks as the climate worsened, but each time a new opportunity arose and people pushed onwards to take advantage of it. Little wonder then, that by 20,000 years ago they had reached the easternmost part of Siberia. From there it was only a small step to the New World.

4

NEW WORLD

● 13,000 years ago

More than twelve millennia before Christopher Columbus landed in the New World, the ancestors of today's native Americans discovered and settled the Americas. Its conquest by these resourceful palaeo-pioneers was the greatest land grab by our species since humans left Africa. What happened when these people met America's monsters?

◀ The first Americans were confronted by more species of bear than existed anywhere else on Earth. This grizzly bear is only one third of the weight of the largest bear it met.

When Worlds Collide

It is worth briefly considering the physical history of the New World, because the landscape and animals that the first explorers met were the consequence of ancient processes that continue to shape the Americas to this day. It helps to understand the world the first palaeo-pioneers discovered, and even the New World today, if we know a little about three important events.

East and West Coast Meet

North America did not exist until the end of the age of the dinosaurs, when a receding sea joined two islands together to form the continent. The eastern island, which stretched from Greenland to northern Florida, had as its spine the old, weathered Appalachian Mountains. The western island, reaching from Alaska to northwest Mexico, was dominated by a younger, more geologically active range of jagged volcanoes we now know as the Rocky Mountains. Between them, covering the Great Plains, lay a shallow sea. The fact that North America was originally composed of two separated islands explains why its eastern and western animals and plants are so different now.

Sixty-five million years ago, a massive asteroid, some 10 km (6 miles) long and travelling at 90,000 km (56,000 miles) per second, slammed into the southern edge of the sea separating eastern and western North America. The collision and its aftermath destroyed most life on Earth. This K-T asteroid, as scientists call it, exterminated the world's dinosaurs and, in doing so, paved the way for mammals and birds to become large. Whereas previously the biggest mammals on Earth were the size of domestic cats, the extinction of the dinosaurs now allowed them to grow to colossal proportions. The collision also created North America's unique vegetation – its conifer and deciduous forests – which evolved from survivors sheltering in its Arctic regions.

About 60 million years ago forces deep within the Earth's crust began to lift the western island and drained the sea over the Great Plains, so that the east and west became the one island we now call North America. This young continent's only connections to the outside world were occasional Arctic land bridges to Asia and, via Greenland, to Europe. About 34 million years ago, the grass family evolved and began to cover the Great Plains, stimulating the evolution of new types of mammals: ruminants (cows, sheep, deer and goats), horses, camels and dogs, all of which subsequently dispersed to Eurasia. Those left behind in North America were eventually outnumbered by successive waves of Eurasian immigrants, like bears, elephants and bison, which radiated into many new forms. These were later replaced by yet newer Eurasian animals.

South America, which had torn free from the ancient supercontinent of Gondwanaland millions of years previously, had drifted aimlessly and alone, but it collided with North America about 2.8 million years ago, creating a land bridge at Panama. Tropical ocean currents that had flowed between the Atlantic and Pacific were now redirected northwards along the east coast of North America, increasing rainfall in the north and so creating the beginnings of a northern ice cap. Around this time North American species like raccoons, mice, skunks, peccaries, horses, dogs, cats, camels and deer invaded South America, while South American species like ground sloths, porcupines, glyptodonts, capybaras and terror-birds expanded north in a great faunal interchange. The unique fauna that the New World's palaeo-explorers would discover was taking shape.

Ice Invasion

By about 2.4 million years ago ice ages began in earnest. Palaeoclimatologists continue to debate their trigger: periodic variation in Earth's orbit, axis wobble, changing configuration of the continents and accompanying ocean currents, varying atmospheric composition and fluctuation in solar radiation have all been proposed. We still do not know the exact cause.

Ice ages wax and wane in periodic cycles, with relatively warm periods (interglacials) between the peaks (glacial maxima). Today we are in the middle of an interglacial. Over the past 2.4 million years, Earth has switched between ice advance and retreat at least 17 times, with these changes sometimes occurring in as little as a human lifetime. The last glacial maximum peaked about 22,500 years ago, and the ice began to retreat about 18,000 years ago. At its peak 80 million cubic km (19 million cubic miles) of sea water were locked away in the world's glaciers and ice sheets, causing the sea level to drop. As a result the Bering Sea between North America and Eurasia became dry land, called the Bering land bridge. Canada and Greenland were buried under a layer of ice 46 per cent larger in area than modern Antarctica. North America has just 0.4 per cent of this ice left today – an indication of just how warm it is now.

▲ Ice sheets up to 2.4 km (1½ miles) thick once covered the northern Rockies. Today this ice has almost entirely melted. Only recently it towered high above these ranges.

The North American ice cap was actually composed of two parts: the larger Laurentide ice sheet covered all of Canada and Greenland east of the Rockies to a depth of up to 3 km (1.9 miles), and a smaller western ice sheet covered British Columbia and southern Alaska to a similar depth. However, some areas, like Beringia (the region around the Bering land bridge) and the Yukon, had such an arid climate with so little snow that they remained ice-free.

By about 15,000 years ago interglacial warming began to expose an ice-free corridor just east of the Rocky Mountains, as well as ice-free areas along the Pacific coast. There were soon to be routes into the New World.

125

The First Americans

Columbus sailed the ocean blue in fourteen hundred and ninety-two.

AMERICAN SCHOOL RHYME

Jared Diamond has pointed out, with some irony, that the United States has two national holidays to celebrate the arrival of Europeans (Columbus Day and Thanksgiving), but none to commemorate the earlier and more spectacular discovery of the Americas by its own indigenous people.

American students could be forgiven for thinking the history of the New World began with Christopher Columbus (and most would probably be shocked to learn that he never even saw the United States). Exceptional students might venture that Basque whalers and the Vikings had landed in the New World a few hundred years earlier than Columbus, but those referring to Native Americans as explorers, pioneers or colonists thousands of years before Columbus would probably be met with confused expressions.

Something prevents us from considering palaeo-Americans in those terms, if we consider them at all. Yet the ancestors of the native Americans discovered and colonized more than a quarter of Earth's land surface, occupying every environment in the Americas in the same amount of time as European pioneers did thousands of years later. Moreover, they colonized North America in the late Pleistocene, when the New World was much colder than it is now, with a more chaotic climate and geology. These people confronted unfamiliar and dangerous animals that were more bountiful than Africa's fauna today, and they invented agriculture on two independent occasions. As Ken Tankersley, anthropologist at Northern Kentucky University, has noted, it will not be until humans successfully colonize the planets that our species will have pioneered a world larger than that found by these first Americans.

So where did the indigenous peoples of the Americas come from, what route did they take to discover these two continents, and when did they first arrive?

Beyond Siberia

The physical appearance of native Americans and South Americans suggests that they originally came from Asia, and recent genetic and linguistic research supports this theory. Studies of native American language families indicate that there were at least three prehistoric waves of colonization from Asia. All the indigenous peoples of Central and South America, and most North American 'Indians', seem to be descendants of the Clovis people, whom many believe to be the oldest, or first wave, of Asian colonists. The Athabascan, or Na-Dene, people who inhabit parts of the American West and the boreal forests of northwest Canada and Alaska, seem to represent a second and later group of immigrants. Archaeological and linguistic evidence suggests that the people speaking the Eskimo and Aleut languages of the far north are even more recent colonists, having arrived only in the last few thousand years.

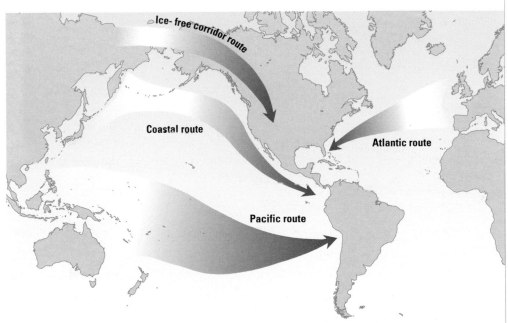

▲ Map showing possible routes by which humans first discovered the New World. Genetic evidence suggests that land or water routes from northern Asia are most likely.

The easiest route to the New World for the first colonists would have been across the Bering Sea. Today this is a journey of 88 km (55 miles) by boat, though it is possible on foot when winter pack ice forms well. In a colder past such ice bridges would have been more common, but through much of prehistory there would have been no need for either boats or hazardous ice crossings – for the Bering Strait was dry land. During the last glacial maximum, 18,000 years ago, global sea levels fell by 91 m (300 feet), exposing the large plains of Beringia between Siberia and Alaska. Beringia was massive, stretching as much as 1,600 km (1,000 miles) from north to south. Although it was cold and dry, this former sea bed was fertile, and grasses, herbs, dwarf birch and willows grew in a peculiar ecological mix known as mammoth steppe. As Earth's climate cooled and warmed over the last 2 million years, the land bridge has emerged and submerged several times, providing clues to a big question: when did the first Americans arrive?

COLD COMFORT

The exploration and settlement of the New World at the end of the Pleistocene would have been impossible without sophisticated cold-weather clothing and shelters. Beringia's brutal climate meant that only the best-equipped pioneers could survive. South of the ice sheets, average temperatures in North America were 7°C (11°F) lower than today, and winter temperatures in places like Tennessee and South Carolina 17°C (29°F) colder than at present. To make matters worse, North America was also much windier, with prevailing northerlies driving frigid air across the continent from the ice cap. Clothing would have been made from tailored animal skins, which would have been windproof when worn in multiple layers. Garment combinations could have been versatile, with the fur facing in or out, or layers could have been removed, according to the weather. European explorers paid with their lives using inferior clothing when trekking through the Canadian Arctic thousands of years later. Today people from all backgrounds use clothing developed by the descendants of the first Americans when visiting Arctic regions.

▶ **The first Americans had advanced cold-weather clothing and weapons that allowed them to discover and colonize the New World.**

Although a land bridge to Alaska provided an obvious route for Asian colonists, there was a cruel catch: such land bridges appear only during severe glacial cold snaps, when life is hardest and when the ice sheets are at their largest and block routes south. In Beringia ice ages acted like a giant airlock, providing a land route to a frozen Alaska, but closing off access to the rest of North America. This is important, because it may help us to pinpoint the date when humans discovered the Americas south of the ice. It also tells us something about the first colonists: to survive in such an inhospitable climate they must have been sophisticated people, with cold-weather clothing and shelters, an adaptable and portable hunting technology, and a highly cooperative social culture. Perhaps this is why no other species of hominid, or even archaic *Homo sapiens*, managed to colonize these lands. The ancestors of today's native Americans were simply the best cold-weather explorers the world had ever known.

The Way South

As the climate started to warm up about 15,000 years ago, an ice-free corridor opened to the east of the Rocky Mountains, providing a route south. This region had always received less snow because it lay in the rain shadow of the mountains, so its thinner ice would have melted first. Other evidence supports the theory: the geology in the corridor region today shows relatively little glacial erosion, and the distribution of animals and plants suggests the area was colonized earlier than neighbouring lands.

Such a corridor would have had a profound ecological impact. For the first time in more than 10,000 years, people and animals could walk south from Alaska and into the great body of the Americas. The ice-free land must at first have been a forbidding sight, strewn with rubble and melting blocks of ice, blasted by cold winds, and riddled with torrential rivers, bogs and infertile lakes. This glacially devastated terrain would have had little edible vegetation or firewood, and probably few resident animals. In some places the pioneers may even have walked unknowingly across the ice sheets, since powerful winds would have blown soil on to them, allowing plants to grow. The first humans to explore the corridor may have been desperate and probably too frightened to enjoy the spectacular scenery. Perhaps the route through the ice was pioneered by migratory animals like caribou, with human hunters later tracking these herds south.

As Earth warmed and glaciers melted, ice-free land also appeared along the Pacific coast of Alaska and British Columbia. Some experts think the first Americans took this route, using boats to travel south along the coast from eastern Beringia. The fact that Asians reached Australia some 60,000 years ago indicates that humans had boats capable of short ocean crossings many thousands of years before the discovery of

▶ Did the first Americans circumvent the ice caps by boating along the coast of Alaska and Canada? Open boats made of animal hides could safely navigate these waters.

the New World. At present we simply do not know which route people used to reach the Americas south of the ice. The likely landing site of immigrants who travelled by boat is today sparsely populated and little explored by archaeologists. There are undoubtedly great archaeological finds still waiting to be discovered along this coast.

When Did Humans Arrive?

If we are unable at present to identify the exact route people took south from Beringia, there is even more controversy surrounding the actual date of arrival and the identity of those who made the breakthrough. We do know that indigenous peoples from Greenland to the southern tip of

THE FIRST AMERICAN INVENTION

Clovis points have been found in every US state below Alaska. These distinctive stone points appear suddenly in the archaeological record about 13,000 years ago and were first discovered near Clovis, New Mexico, in the 1930s. Looking like spearheads, Clovis points were usually attached to a long dart shaft and launched with an atlatl (see page 136). They were used for hunting large animals, often being found with, or even embedded in, the bones of mammoths. They have a unique grooved or fluted shape that is

▶ Clovis technology was complex and deadly. The Clovis point on top is for killing megafauna. It and other tools were made from one easy-to-carry, partially shaped block (beneath).

South America are more similar to one another, both physically and genetically, than are the indigenous peoples of any other continent. This indicates that they arrived more recently and have had less time to diversify than the native peoples of Africa, Australia or Eurasia. But when exactly did the first Americans arrive?

Archaeologists are divided into two camps regarding both the timing of the New World's discovery and the identity of the colonists. A smaller 'Clovis first' group believes that the Clovis people, whose distinctive stone artefacts were first discovered in Clovis, New Mexico, were the first humans to discover and colonize the Americas, about 13,000 years ago. A larger group thinks there were pre-Clovis colonists hundreds or even thousands of years earlier. The issue has been one the most important and contentious in New World archaeology. Knowing the date of arrival is

remarkably uniform throughout the vast area over which they are found, suggesting that they were made by a pioneering culture. The grooves helped secure the points to shafts, and also caused victims to bleed more profusely. The points were made of high-quality, sometimes semiprecious, stones like chert, quartz, obsidian, flint and hematite and often shattered once inside their victims, maximizing damage. They form the basis of a light and highly mobile tool kit, with off-cuts from their manufacture being used for a variety of other tools. For example, final shaping of a point created razor-sharp flakes needed for butchering animals and scraping hides, while earlier shaping produced knives and hide scrapers. Great skill was needed

▲ The first Americans made tools that were beautiful and functional. Surprisingly sharp Clovis blades have even been used to perform surgical operations.

to make these tools – and only a handful of archaeologists have managed to reproduce them to a comparable quality. The deadly Clovis point has been called the 'first American invention'.

important because it tells us how long people lived with the New World megafauna, and whether they had a role in their demise.

Despite years of research, evidence for pre-Clovis sites remains inconclusive. As Tim Flannery of the Museum of South Australia has noted, New World archaeology is littered with sites initially thought to be pre-Clovis, such as Calico, Louisville, Texas Street and others, but since shown to have been misdated. Some pre-Clovis claims, such as Sandia Cave, may even be fakes. But there are several sites that have been repeatedly dated as much older than 13,000 years. The best documented of these is the Monte Verde site in southern Chile, excavated by a team of archaeologists led by Tom Dillehay of the University of Kentucky.

At Monte Verde, the remains of a strange, elephant-like gomphothere (*Cuvieronius*) were found together with wooden and stone tools, human footprints and megafaunal remains. Monte Verde's preservation is excellent because the site was buried under a layer of peat soon after people abandoned it. Radiocarbon tests on wood and bone from the site suggest that it dates from between 14,800 and 14,400 years ago – more than a thousand years before Clovis. Other dates published by the same group of researchers suggest that humans occupied nearby sites more than 30,000 years ago. If these dates are correct, humans were in the New World many thousands of years before the Clovis people.

However, there are reasons to believe that sites regarded as pre-Clovis may be dated incorrectly. Consider the pattern of colonization that might be expected if modern humans, already capable of thriving in the cold of Siberia, invaded a virgin world with a gentle climate, vast numbers of naïve game animals, and no human diseases or competitors. Would we expect small numbers of colonists to struggle at low density for thousands of years in game-rich paradises like California and Florida, leaving little trace of themselves except in a few widely scattered locations? This is what pre-Clovis supporters are proposing. But the history of human

◄ **The Clovis discovered one quarter of Earth's land surface. Not until we pioneer life on other planets will our species acquire such territory again. This Clovis man is holding an atlatl dart.**

(and animal) invasions suggests that, in such conditions, there would be a sudden and rapid expansion and dispersal of the human population, leading to a uniform technology spread across a large area. This initial boom would perhaps be followed by a crash, as the environment became saturated, followed in turn by a period of readjustment. The scenario fits the pattern for Clovis culture. Their distinctive projectile points appear

THE ATLATL

Atlatls are stick- or board-shaped wooden and bone spear-throwers used by early Americans. They were put to deadly effect by the first Americans, who used them to launch high-speed darts, tipped with stone Clovis points, at New World megafauna.

Atlatls are easy to use and allow weapons to be thrown with more power than conventional spears, because they give the thrower's arm extra leverage. The stone-tipped dart lies alongside the atlatl, with the dart base fitting in a hooked notch at one end. The pair are gripped in one hand and thrown with a whipping action. As the dart is released, the atlatl bends and then springs back into shape providing extra propulsion. This more than doubles the force that could be provided just by throwing a spear.

Equipped with this deadly weapon, early Americans could puncture the tough hides of mammoths and other monsters to inflict mortal wounds from a safe distance. They may also have used the weapon against each other. The Aztecs (descendants of

▲ Their atlatl and dart technology allowed the Clovis to hunt America's monsters.

the Clovis) in Mexico had an entire army outfitted with atlatls, and depictions of atlatl warriors appear at the entrance of one Aztec stadium. Today practised throwers can repeatedly hit a target the size of a grapefruit from nearly 40 m (130 feet) away, and the world record throw is 258 m (846 feet).

suddenly in the archaeological record, spread rapidly, but last for only a few hundred years – all the hallmarks of pioneers occupying a virgin world. Although 'Clovis First' is a minority view, no one denies that these people are the first recognizable New World culture.

Pre-Clovis proponents argue that signs of earlier people are elusive because their technology was less sophisticated than that of Clovis tools, and because the early colonists lived at the height of the Ice age in a climate that was, on average, colder and drier. This less productive world would have supported fewer people, so there are fewer archaeological sites. However, even at the peak of the Ice age, many parts of the New World were ideal for humans. As Tim Flannery points out, Australia had a similar cool, dry, Ice-age climate 20,000–40,000 years ago, yet there is lots of evidence of human occupation during that period, despite poorer conditions for artefact preservation. Why should the New World be different? It seems hard to explain how a widespread pre-Clovis population could leave so little evidence of its existence.

If the Clovis people really were the first Americans, why are claims of pre-Clovis discoveries so common? Ken Tankersley thinks one reason is the influence of the media. Archaeology is a more public science than other disciplines. In chemistry, physics and biology, debate takes place mainly in journals and at conferences, with results peer-reviewed before media notification. Archaeology is different. It is one of the few sciences where new discoveries are funded, and sometimes even accompanied, by the media. What other science has film crews present at the moment of discovery, as at recent Inca mummy digs? Pre-Clovis claims simply make better stories and are more likely to intrigue the public. A second reason such finds are common is archaeologists' desire to push back the boundaries of science and find ever earlier sites. Consider the pattern of discovery we would expect to see if the first wave of colonization had been correctly identified, but scientists continued striving for older sites. Every year we would hear of exciting but controversial claims that older sites had been found, only for subsequent researchers to reveal, with far less fanfare, that they had been wrongly dated. This appears be the pattern we see today in New World archaeology.

It seems wisest to be cautious about pre-Clovis claims until independent investigators have verified them, so for the rest of this chapter we will assume that the Clovis people were the first Americans. However, there is one thing that everyone agrees on: when the first people did arrive, they encountered some incredible animals.

America's Monsters

It is hard to convey just how amazing, untamed and different were the creatures that confronted the first palaeo-explorers as they travelled south from the ice caps at the end of the Pleistocene. In stark contrast, so little of the American megafauna now remains that to see a large animal in the wild is a rare and often moving experience. Although natural history documentaries give the impression that bears, pumas and moose lurk behind every tree, the truth is that the only native megafaunal species most North Americans are likely to see outside captivity is one genus of

BEAR ATTACK!

Arctodus simus, the giant short-faced bear, was the largest mammalian land carnivore ever to have walked the Earth. Males weighed up to 1,000 kg (2,205 lb), or three times more than an a grizzly bear. They measured 1.5 m (5 feet) at the shoulder, 3.4 m (11 feet) high when standing on their hind legs and could reach 1.4 m (5 feet) above a basketball hoop. Although technically a bear, its strange anatomy and scavenging lifestyle means it is more accurate to picture it as a 'horse-sized hyena'. Long legs and forward-pointing feet enabled it to trot at speed, rather than waddling like modern bears, and a gigantic nose allowed it to sniff out hunters' carcasses from great distances. Its teeth functioned like opposing sledgehammers, giving it an exceptionally powerful bite that could crack megafaunal bones to access the fatty marrow inside. It was probably the most terrifying creature that humans ever met.

▶ **Horse-sized *Arctodus* was such a powerful opponent that it may well have delayed human colonization of the New World. It evolved to dominate animal kills.**

deer (*Odocoileus*). In South America your chance of seeing large animals is even slimmer. The living bears, camelids, pigs, moose, wolves, caribou, sheep, goats, muskoxen, tapirs and big cats of the New World are so rare, and seen by so few people outside captivity, that they might as well be as dead as mammoths and sabre-tooths. What is even stranger is that large expanses of suitable habitat still exist, but they are mostly empty. Less than a quarter of the different types of New World megafauna that the palaeo-pioneers met are alive today. Drive to the last wild areas of North America's Great Plains, and they are silent. Canoe through the vast and spooky coniferous forests of Canada or the Amazon, and they are comparatively empty. There is food there – trees, marshes, grasslands, teeming with small mammals, birds, amphibians and insects – yet there are very few large animals.

In some respects the New World of the Pleistocene was just like the New World of today. Nearly all of the plants, small animals and insects that currently dominate these lands today were also dominant then. Fossil evidence tells us that the first Americans saw the same squirrels,

WOOLLY MAMMOTH

Mammuthus primigenius is the most famous of the Americas' five species of elephant. It lived in the Arctic tundra in the margins of coniferous forests during Clovis times. It was smaller than other elephants, rarely measuring more than 2.7 m (9 feet) tall and weighing up to 8 tons. Frozen remains reveal that it had a dense coat of dark brown to almost black hair, and an undercoat of wool 10 cm (4 inches) thick. Mammoth wool would have protected the animal against extreme cold, as did its relatively small ears and short trunk. Other distinctive features included a knob-like dome on the head and a sloping back bearing a fat-filled hump.

Like all mammoths, woolly mammoths were grazers, with grinding teeth specialized for breaking down grasses and sedges. They spent perhaps 12 hours a day gathering an estimated 180 kg (400 lb) in food which they plucked from the ground with their trunk tips. Unlike living elephants, woolly mammoths inhabited an area that was covered in snow for part of the year, and this may have forced them to migrate long distances.

The remains of woolly mammoths have been found from Britain through to Siberia, and ice-free Canada and the USA. The species was widespread in North America but became extinct in the late Pleistocene, with an isolated population surviving on Wrangel Island in the Russian Arctic until 4,000 years ago, when the Egyptians were building pyramids.

▼ **The woolly mammoth disappeared comparatively recently. Its nearest living relative is the Indian elephant.**

raccoons, maple trees, cacti and butterflies that North Americans live with now, albeit in slightly different locations. But there was one major difference, for fossils also reveal that the first Americans set eyes on some of the most amazing wildlife spectacles the world has ever seen. As they explored the Americas they encountered herds of giant animals more abundant, varied and strange than in any African game park. They discovered an American Serengeti.

MASTODON

Mammut americanum was only distantly related to modern elephants and arrived in the New World 17 million years ago. Mastodons were lighter than mammoths, growing to about 2.5–3 m (8–10 feet) tall and 4–6 tons in weight. They preferred woodlands and may have lived in smaller herds than their cousins. Their teeth indicate they were browsers – plant-eaters that fed on trees and shrubs rather than grass – and, like living elephants, they would have shaped the landscape. Mastodon dung and gut contents have been found so well preserved that the dormant microbes within them have been brought back to life. The best modern analogues for mastodon feeding are probably giraffes or moose. Clovis points embedded in mastodon bone indicate they were prey for Clovis settlers.

▼ **Mastodons were smaller than mammoths and preferred to browse in woodland areas.**

COLUMBIAN MAMMOTH

This gigantic and close relative of the woolly mammoth was one of the most impressive sights on the New World prairies. Columbian mammoths (*Mammuthus columbi*) were perhaps the largest elephants ever to have lived. Measuring up to 4 m (13 feet) at the shoulder and weighing 10 tons – much larger than African elephants today – they would have had to eat around 225 kg (500 lb) of grasses and sedges each day, supplemented with tender spruce tips, oak leaves, sagebrush, cattails and even prickly pear cacti, all of which have been found in their dung.

Columbian mammoths were less hairy than woolly mammoths and had longer, more curved tusks. They arrived from Asia only 1.7 million years ago, and their remains and dung have been found in dry caves, which they may have used as salt licks. They thrived in deserts, grasslands and parkland environments. Their tusks, which grew up to 4.5 m (15 feet) long, are thought to have served a social function as well as providing defence against predators. One Columbian mammoth cow would provide Clovis hunters with about 2 tons of meat and fat.

▼ **The prehistoric Americas had more elephants than anywhere else on Earth – often five per square mile.**

Hairy Giants

Today African grasslands can support nearly 30 tons of large mammals per square mile. The Pleistocene Serengetis of the Americas may well have teemed with megafaunal herds just as massive. And Serengeti is the right word – like humans, many of the New World's animals had African origins and emigrated to the Americas via the Bering land bridge. Among the most striking were mighty prehistoric elephants, such as mastodons, which entered the New World some 17 million years ago. We now think of elephants as African or Asian animals, yet in the recent past the Americas were home to at least five species – more than anywhere else.

There are around 30 sites where archaeologists have found evidence that early Americans hunted elephants. Since most are near water, where remains are more likely to become preserved, it seems likely that we have underestimated the prevalence of elephant hunting. The first humans to enter the New World had thousands of years of mammoth-hunting experience behind them, so they probably arrived already equipped with the tools and skills needed to bring down these huge animals.

Ice-age Kentucky Derby

Once the shock of seeing elephants and other giants had worn off, palaeo-pioneers would have noticed an appetizing selection of hoofed mammals. Most schoolchildren learn that the horse was introduced to the Americas by the Spanish, but fewer know that the horse family originally evolved in North America and only subsequently migrated to the rest of the world. The first Americans discovered at least five species of horse roaming the grasslands and tundra thousands of years before the Spanish

▶ American bison (*Bison bison*) are recent immigrants from Eurasia that walked into the New World with the first Americans. Palaeo-colonists discovered landscapes filled with animals.

143

arrived. Some reconstructions of these horses show them with zebra-like stripes, a characteristic that has deep roots in the horse family. Africa's zebras are actually descendants of American horses.

Alongside the horses were camels. They also evolved in the New World and were specialists in coping with changeable and arid environments. The first Americans discovered several unique, llama-like camels living in North America, as well as the huge Yesterday's camel (*Camelops hesternus*), a cold-adapted, one-humped version with legs 20 per cent longer than those of any living camel. Yesterday's camel bones have been found at 18 Clovis sites, and one of the bones had been fashioned into a tool. These days only two wild species of camel survive in the Americas (the vicuña and guanaco – close relatives of domestic llamas and alpacas), and they are now restricted to the Andes.

Other distinctive hoofed mammals trapped behind the ice caps included an archaic form of moose with strange antlers, a type of woodland muskox, a weird mountain goat, strange antelopes, pigs, tapirs and long-horned bison. These now-extinct creatures, together with hoofed mammals that still exist, created a Serengeti-like community on the grassy plains. The long-horned bison (*Bison antiquus*) were larger than today's buffalo and had larger, straighter horns with a span of more than 2 m (7 feet) between the tips. They may have played an ecological role similar to that of Cape buffalo in Africa today. And just as buffalo sometimes fall prey to lions, so did long-horned bison – a mummified corpse of one of these animals was found in Alaska with a tooth fragment from an American lion (*Panthera atrox*) lodged in its body.

Monsters at War

The plant-eaters were potential prey for a huge range of carnivores. The Americas of the Pleistocene boasted an impressive suite of big cats, including some of the largest the world has seen. Among them was the American sabre-tooth (*Smilodon fatalis*); the American scimitar (*Homotherium serum*); the American lion, which at up to 500 kg (1,100 lb)

AMERICAN SABRE-TOOTH

Smilodon fatalis is one of the largest cats ever known. It stood 1.2 m (4 feet) at the shoulder and weighed up to 340 kg (740 lb). Its most distinctive feature is the gigantic canine teeth that grew to 18 cm (7 inches) long, which helped it to kill other megafauna. *Smilodon* probably ambushed its prey using its 'sabres' to slice deep, gaping wounds in prey, causing them to bleed to death. Though the teeth were effective killing weapons, they probably got in the way during feeding and may also have been used as social or sexual signals to other sabre-tooths. There are hundreds of beautifully preserved fossils of these animals from the La Brea tar pits in Los Angeles.

▼ Giant teeth made this cat a specialized predator of megafauna too large for American lions. It was once common throughout the Americas.

was twice the weight of modern African lions; and even an American cheetah (*Miracinonyx trumani*). The cheetah was one of the only cat genera that originated in North America. It spread to the Old World via the Bering land bridge and found its way to Africa about 1–2 million years ago, where its descendants survive to this day; the small head and long tail of Africa's cheetah betray its close relationship with the cougar.

If lions, sabre-toothed cats and cougars were not enough, North America was also home to lynxes and bobcats, as well as many cats now restricted to the tropics, including jaguars, ocelots, jaguarundis, river

ELEPHANT-SLAYER

Homotherium serum, the American scimitar cat, is named after its strange, serrated canine teeth, which formed terrifying slicing weapons rather like steak knives. It was smaller than the American lion, measuring 1.1 m (3½ feet) at the shoulder and weighing 150–250 kg (330–550 lb), but its build was more like a hyena's, with slender front legs and shorter hind legs. Its claws were semi-retractable, like a cheetah's, suggesting it was a fast runner. The bones of 30 adult scimitars and two kittens were found in a Texas cave, along with the gnawed remains of 400 mammoths, most of which were around two years old. It seems *Homotherium* specialized in killing young elephants, waiting for them to become distanced from their mothers or herds

before striking. The cat's teeth were designed for ripping through elephant hides. Fossils indicate that it carried food back to its den. It is possible that it hunted in prides, using teamwork to separate young mammoths from their parents.

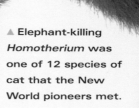

▲ Elephant-killing *Homotherium* was one of 12 species of cat that the New World pioneers met.

cats and margays. Nowhere else in the world did such a diverse range of cats live together at one time. That so many could coexist suggests that the New World's grasslands must have teemed with vast numbers of plant-eaters.

Alongside the cats lived today's grey wolf, red wolf and coyote, as well as the extinct dire wolf (*Canis dirus*). But dwarfing all the dogs and cats were seven species of New World bear. The first that humans would have met was the giant short-faced bear (*Arctodus simus*) – the largest mammalian carnivore known to science. It was such a terrifying size that some scientists think its presence may have delayed the arrival of humans in North America.

The abundance of predators and prey created a role for huge scavengers, and the horse-sized giant short-faced bear was the biggest. It used an enormous, sensitive nose to sniff out carrion, sheer strength to drive predators from their kills, and bone-cracking jaws to feed on the leftovers. The first Americans must have lived in fear of it – their hunts would have attracted its attention, and it may well have forced them to butcher animals wastefully and move on. Fortunately for present-day hikers and campers, this nightmarish animal is now extinct.

Another indication of the African-like abundance of animals was a frightening assemblage of vultures and eagles. These included the teratorns – the largest birds to have flown Earth's skies. The teratorns evolved in South America and later invaded North America. The largest North American species was the incredible teratorn (*Teratornis incredibilis*), which had a wingspan of nearly 5 m (16 feet) – twice that of any living bird. But even this bird was a dwarf compared to its South American relative, the magnificent teratorn (*Argentavis magnificens*), whose wingspan of up to 12 m (39 feet) made it the size of a small aeroplane. Scientists are puzzled by these huge birds: were they predators or just giant garbage-disposal machines? We still don't know for certain. Along with the teratorns flew many now-extinct species of vulture, eagle, hawk and owl. Animal carcasses on the plains of Pleistocene America must have been smothered with squabbling masses of feathered monsters.

PLEISTOCENE SURVIVOR

The Californian condor (*Gymnogyps californianus*) is the sole surviving relic of a group of giant scavenging birds that flourished in the Americas thanks to the abundant monster predators. Today it is one of the rarest (and largest) birds in the world, weighing 10 kg (22 lb) with a wingspan of 2.9 m (9 feet). It dates back to the Middle Pleistocene when it ranged widely over North America. Bones, eggshells and feathers have been found in caves in Arizona, west Texas and New Mexico, and show that the Grand Canyon was a particularly important nesting area. There is even evidence that the condor fed on mastodons in New York State during Clovis times.

The condor's demise and the disappearance of a suite of scavenging relatives coincided with the extinction of the Pleistocene megafauna.

When Europeans arrived, *Gymnogyps* remained only along the Pacific coast, surviving on dead marine mammals. By the early 1700s domestic animals had replaced its extinct megafaunal food and it re-invaded some of its former range in western North America. Since then poisoning programmes, egg collecting, wire collisions and shooting have decimated its numbers. On 19 April 1987 the last wild birds were taken into captivity in California in an attempt to save them. Two small wild populations and one captive population have now been established and condors are flying once more in the Grand Canyon, perhaps for the first time in 10,000 years.

▼ **Andean condors are relics of a group of feathered scavengers from the Ice age. Persecution has driven their Californian cousins to the brink of extinction.**

Monsters Vanish

At the end of the Pleistocene the New World's megafauna was devastated by a mysterious mass extinction. In less than 3,000 years, some 40 genera of large animal became extinct, whereas only nine had disappeared in the previous 70,000 years. This extinction is one of the most puzzling in our planet's history, and its importance has not been fully recognized. Forces that can exterminate so many animals so quickly have the potential to threaten human survival, yet we learn nothing about the megafaunal extinctions at school, and we spend very little research money investigating them.

Many theories have been proposed, including global epidemics, cosmic events, climate change and overkill by human hunters. These last two theories are favoured by the majority of scientists who have debated the issue, and opinion is sharply divided into two rival camps. One fact upon which there is general agreement is that mass extinctions have occurred many times in the New World's history, with at least seven in the last 10 million years. The first six of these seem to be associated with climate change, but the last, which was the most serious, may have had a different cause. Exploring a few simple questions can help us to shed light on this mystery.

What kinds of animals became extinct? In North America 73 per cent of animal genera weighing more than 44 kg (97 lb) disappeared, but only about five small victims are known. In South America an astounding 80 per cent of megafauna genera died out, but again few small animals disappeared. This is strange because previous mass extinctions affected a broader range of body sizes, not just megafauna.

Climate change is a global phenomenon, so we would expect climate-induced extinctions to happen simultaneously in different continents. But while the North and South American mass extinctions happened at about the same time, Australia's occurred much earlier, Polynesia's was 10,000 years later, and the extinctions in Eurasia and Africa occurred earlier, over a longer period, and less extensively. The fact that the extinctions were not simultaneous suggests climate was not the sole cause of the monster extinctions in the Americas.

Another puzzling feature is that none of the previous extinction events happened during a warming period, but the end-Pleistocene New World extinctions did. It seems hard for the climate theory to explain why both heat-adapted (glyptodonts and tapirs) and cold-adapted (Harrington's mountain goat and shrub oxen) species should perish when a general warming was creating new, ice-free habitats. Also difficult to explain is why megafauna on islands should persist longer than their counterparts on nearby mainland. Cuban ground sloths, for instance, disappeared more than 4,000 years later than their mainland cousins, and a relict population of mammoths survived on remote Wrangel Island until 4,000 years ago. These facts do begin to make sense if you consider the possibility that humans were involved.

Monster Hunters?

Could there be clues to the New World's megafaunal extinctions in the culture of the first Americans? Several features of the Clovis people implicate them. The first is their remarkable brevity: their large, fluted projectile points, designed for hunting large animals, lasted for only about 300 years, after which they were replaced by smaller weapons called Folsom points. Folsom points are usually associated with the bones of extinct bison – never with the mammoths preferred by Clovis hunters. One obvious explanation is that, as mammoths became rare, Clovis points became obsolete. Clovis points show relatively little regional variation, which suggests they were made by a pioneer culture that swept quickly through the New World. Such rapid expansion suggests an abundance of food.

Proponents of the climate theory find it hard to believe that a small band of hunters could breed and move fast enough to populate the whole of North and South America in just 1,000 years. Overkill theorists, such as Paul Martin of the University of Arizona, counter that there are historical examples of human populations growing by 3.4 per cent a year in

GROUND SLOTHS

About 7 million years ago monsters from South America swam to North America. Ground sloths were among the strangest animals that early Americans met. There were five species, ranging from lion-sized to giants as tall as giraffes. Each was apparently specialized for a certain habitat and type of plant food. Rusconi's ground sloth (*Eremotherium rusconii*), found as far north as the southeastern USA, was a 6-m (20-foot)-long, 3-ton monster with shaggy fur, armoured skin and claws nearly 0.5 m (20 inches) long. Other ox-sized species were cold-adapted and lived as far north as Alaska, where they browsed on shrubs and other plants.

Ground sloths could raise themselves on to trunk-like hind legs, allowing them to feed among trees and ward off the New World's impressive line-up of predators. The remains of some individuals are so well preserved that tendons and skin are still present, and the dung smells fresh when moistened. Examination of the dung of Shasta's ground sloth (*Nothrotheriops shastense*), found in a cave in the American southwest, indicates that this 180-kg (400-lb) individual ate Mormon tea, globe mallow and mustard plants, which are still found in the region today. The sloth family evolved in the Americas, but the only surviving members are five small tree-dwelling species that are confined to the relative safety of Central and South America's jungles.

▼ **Rusconi's ground sloth (*Eremotherium rusconii*) was an elephant-sized monster. Was it hunted to extinction by the first American pioneers?**

virgin lands with plentiful resources – a plausible scenario in the Pleistocene New World, where there were no endemic human diseases or human competitors to limit population growth. At that growth rate, 100 explorers would give rise to 10 million descendants in only 340 years. And the pioneers need only have advanced 13 km (8 miles) a year to cover the 12,800 km (8,000 miles) from Edmonton, Alberta, to Tierra del Fuego at the southern tip of South America.

That early Americans hunted mammoths is beyond question. Many New World sites showing evidence of mammoth hunting have been

TO KILL A MAMMOTH

It seems inconceivable that prehistoric people could kill elephants, but even in recent times African hunter-gatherers did just that. One of their favourite strategies was to 'wound and track', stalking within a few feet, spearing the animal, and then tracking it until it became weak enough to kill. Wounded elephants often head for water, which might also explain why most mammoth kills are found near water. The Clovis may have used this monster-hunting technique with their powerful atlatls at short range.

A second possible strategy was to drive elephants into soft ground where they got stuck. At Lange Ferguson, South Dakota, a mother and baby mammoth seem to have been killed after getting mired in a bog, while at Colby, Wyoming, mammoths appear to have been caught in deep snow. At Dent in Colorado a whole herd seems to have been trapped in a steep-sided gulley. Mammoth

▲ **Many mammoth skeletons have been found together with Clovis points, indicating that early settlers battled with at least some monsters.**

hunters may have constructed giant traps to catch their quarry. According to the folklore of the Yukon's indigenous people, their ancestors snared mammoths with leather ropes strung between specially weakened trees to entangle them.

found, and some of these (including Clovis, New Mexico; Murray Springs, Arizona; and Colby, Wyoming) contained piles of disarticulated bones, indicating that the animals were deliberately butchered, perhaps to provide winter meat caches. Though there is more evidence of mammoth usage in Eurasia than in the Americas, this perhaps reflects the greater number of archaeological digs in the Old World. It seems likely that there are many more kill sites waiting to be discovered.

Climate proponents point out that there is little evidence of hunting of megafauna other than elephants and the extinct bison, but this might be partly explained by the relatively short time for which humans and New World monsters lived together. If the extinctions happened quickly, evidence would be scarce, since fossilization is a rare process anyway. Even so, verification that other species were hunted does exist. Such evidence includes extinct horse protein embedded in the surface of a Clovis point, tool marks on a camel bone, and even a Clovis point lodged in the jaw of a dire wolf.

MONSTER MERMAID

While most American monsters disappeared soon after the arrival of humans, the Steller's sea cow (*Hydrodamalis gigas*) survived until recently. This huge siren grew fat on a diet of marine plants, with the larger females being up to 8 m (26 feet) long and weighing 10 tons, dwarfing their modern relative the dugong. During the Pleistocene Steller's sea cow was widespread on the Pacific coast from California to Japan. After human arrival its range dwindled, until only a tiny population remained on the uninhabited Komandorskie Islands in the Bering Sea. It was discovered by the European

▲ A dugong, surviving relative of the Steller's sea cow. Sea cows were common along the west coast of North America. The last one died over 200 years ago in Alaska.

explorer Georg Steller in 1768. Within only 27 years it had been hunted to extinction.

▲ The moose (*Alces alces*), like most of the surviving monsters, is a recent immigrant from Eurasia. It arrived with the first Americans and thus had experience of human hunters.

But how could Clovis hunters kill so many large animals in such a short time? The answer may lie in the animals' unfamiliarity with humans. As Georg Steller discovered, the giant Steller's sea cow was so trusting with humans that it was tame enough to touch; the New World's megafauna, with no experience of human weapons or hunting techniques, may have been just as vulnerable. When the first people arrived in North America, they would have had a field day. The few megafaunal species that survived the slaughter were those that were either difficult to track or already used to humans. Moose (elks) and bison, for instance, entered the continent at the same time as the Clovis people and had already coexisted with humans; caribou and pronghorns had unpredictable migrations and were hard to follow. But others had no such luck. And as the great herds of plant-eating mammals disappeared, so too did the predators and scavengers that fed upon them.

▲ The pronghorn (*Antilocapra americana*) is the only truly native North American hoofed animal to survive humans. Is its world-class speed and endurance due to missing predators?

Palaeolithic people are frequently portrayed as primitive, rug-wearing cavemen, but nothing could be further from the truth. We now know that the ancestors of today's native Americans were as anatomically and cognitively modern as any people alive today. To survive in the harsh climate of the far north, they needed sophisticated clothing and hunting technologies. Archaeologists believe that Clovis people were the most mobile hunter-gatherers the world has ever known, and their beautiful but deadly stone points have been found in every environment from seashore caves to mountain tops – a testament to their success.

Despite their advanced society, rapid spread and enormous impact, the Clovis people enjoyed a brief heyday, and left little tangible evidence of themselves. Only one site has yielded human remains: those of a young child, buried – inexplicably – with hundreds of Clovis points on a bleak Montana hillside. Did this represent the dying days of the Clovis culture?

5

ISLANDS

● 5,500–300 years ago

Five millennia before the birth of Captain Cook a small band of stone-age seafarers set out from the island of Taiwan into the unknown. Without compasses or metal tools these Neolithic mariners conquered over half the globe. They were the greatest explorers the world has known and their Pacific Ocean voyages brought them face to face with monsters that became the basis of myth and legend.

◀ Beware dragons! Islands are often home to strange animals found nowhere else on Earth.

Komodo dragons are the world's largest lizards and live only on a few Indonesian islands.

The Polynesians

Today the descendants of Taiwanese explorers – the Polynesians – can be found across the globe from Madagascar to Easter Island and from Hawaii to New Zealand. It is a testament to the courage and skill of these early voyagers that they did not walk to their new homes. Instead, they looked beyond the prows of their canoes to an uncertain future, thousands of miles across unknown waters. Their explorations of the oceans were no less ambitious than our modern attempts to explore the solar system. For the Polynesians islands were like planets, scattered across an endless cosmos of blue ocean.

They discovered more than a million islands, each with a unique ecosystem containing species found nowhere else on Earth; no other stone-age people met such natural diversity. Inherent in the ecology of

▲ Polynesians discovered over a million islands. Most were not idyllic paradises as they lacked many natural resources, so the discovery of large animals and birds was celebrated.

these remote islands was a propensity for unique monsters to evolve. Isolated in tiny worlds, the island megafauna gave rise to some of the most incredible animals ever to greet human eyes.

The conquest of the Polynesian world is the final chapter in a story that began 100,000 years ago, when the first *Homo sapiens* migrated out of Africa to discover new worlds. The Polynesians colonized the last pristine lands on the planet. So recent were their discoveries that they took place within recorded history, and this fact can help us answer an important question: was it humans or some other force that killed the megafauna? The Polynesians give us a clear picture of what happens to an ecosystem when people first arrive. Their exploits were a type of natural scientific experiment, repeated many times over.

Polynesian Origins

For a long time scholars had few clues to the origins of the Polynesians. It is only in the last 30 years that scientists from a variety of fields, including archaeology, human genetics and linguistics, have come to realize that the people of Madagascar and the Pacific islands originally came from Southeast Asia. Through this research has emerged an astounding map charting the routes these people took as they island-hopped across the globe.

Once the scientists had established the Polynesians' origins in Taiwan, they could begin to attach dates to the various voyages by examining archaeological evidence. Beginning in around 3500 BC, a distinctive set of stone tools appeared in Taiwan, as well as a type of pottery called *ta-p'en-k'eng*. Remains of rice and millet reveal a people involved in agriculture, with fish-hooks, stone net-sinkers and adzes for carving canoes showing that they were also accomplished fishermen.

By 1600 BC, similar artefacts had appeared in coastal Papua New Guinea. There was the same distinctive tool kit, along with giant clam shells, tattoo needles, shell fish-hooks and ornamental rings, but now the *ta-p'en-k'eng* pottery had evolved into a new form – Lapita pottery – with finely patterned horizontal bands. It was here that a fully formed culture

PIONEER TONGUES

The languages spoken in Madagascar, Polynesia, Micronesia, coastal Melanesia and parts of Southeast Asia belong to one group: the Austronesian language family. Until recently these languages enjoyed the widest geographical range of any linguistic family in the world. By comparing elements of languages and dialects within the family, linguists have been able to trace the origins of Austronesian tongues. Malagasy (the Madagascan language), for example, has some East African Bantu words, but most of the vocabulary and grammar is Austronesian. Astonishingly, its closest linguistic relative is the language spoken by the Dayak tribe, a community that lives 4,500 km (2,800 miles) away on the island of Borneo.

▲ The Polynesians were the greatest ocean navigators the world has known. They explored over half the globe without magnetic compasses in huge double-hulled, sea-going canoes.

of ocean explorers finally established itself. Eventually Lapita pottery would also disappear, but its geometric designs continued to migrate with the seafarers in the form of tattoos.

The Polynesians transported not only themselves but also their Southeast Asian landscape. This environmental package included many useful plants, such as taro, yams, bananas and a variety of tree species such as almond, Malay apple, breadfruit and coconut. These were not just sources of food – paper mulberry, for example, was used for creating tapa cloth. They also brought domesticated Asian animals, such as chickens, pigs, dogs and the highly valued Pacific rat (*Rattus exulans*).

Ocean Racers

The Lapita mariners accomplished the fastest-known migration in prehistory, averaging 80 km (50 miles) per generation. Radiocarbon dating of Lapita pots reveals that colonists crossed 4,500 km (2,800 miles) of ocean in only 300–500 years. It is clear, therefore, that these people were purposely searching out new islands, not stumbling across them by accident. As they moved, new cultures evolved, and evidence

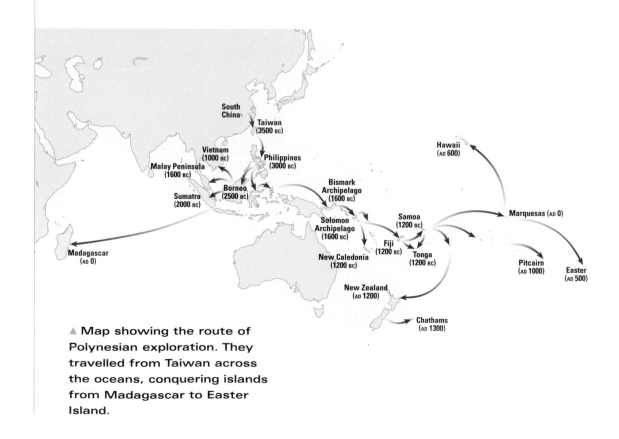

▲ Map showing the route of Polynesian exploration. They travelled from Taiwan across the oceans, conquering islands from Madagascar to Easter Island.

suggests that their innovations spread mainly outwards, rather than passing back towards former homelands.

What motives impelled these people to keep exploring uncharted waters? Some scholars think expanding populations may have forced people to move on as their fragile islands began to run out of natural resources. But the pioneers often appear to have departed before their island homes reached saturation point. The social structure of modern Polynesian cultures provides clues. In Pacific societies great emphasis is placed upon social status, and the highest rank was always accorded to the family of the founding member. Perhaps people wanted to start their own communities, setting up themselves as leader. Or maybe they yearned for an island Eden with unlimited resources. Throughout the Pacific ancient songs celebrate ancestral homelands to the west and wistfully dream of fabled lands of plenty lying just beyond the rising sun to the east.

TA MOKO TATTOOS

Polynesians saw reptiles as magical creatures with links to the underworld. The king of reptiles was the god Moko, a protector of fishermen. In New Zealand and Hawaii people decorated their bodies with Moko tattoos ('tattoo' is a Polynesian word) to produce raised designs like reptilian skin. The Moko tattoos of New Zealand's chieftains were so highly prized that their heads were decapitated and preserved after they died.

▶ Ta Moko facial tattoos were carved into the skin. Worn only by people of high rank, Moko was a *tapu*, or sacred art, whose designs identified the wearer's family history.

Central Pacific

Animals of the Pacific evolved on some of the planet's youngest land. Most of the million or so islands scattered across this ocean had violent volcanic beginnings. As tectonic plates rubbed together and bulbs of magma welled up from the Earth's core, new islands rose from the seabed, creating geographically isolated havens in which unique creatures could evolve.

The volcanic islands emerged from the water as barren rocks, devoid of life, but they were soon colonized. El Niño and cyclones may bring death to some parts of the world, but they also play an important role in transporting life to remote lands. Strong winds blow birds off course, drag insects into air currents, and rip trees from their roots, setting them adrift – occasionally with reptiles and mammals hidden among the branches. Land animals sometimes crossed thousands of miles of ocean to

A BIRD THAT CANNOT FLY

The Henderson rail (*Porzana ater*) is the only surviving flightless bird in eastern Polynesia. Henderson Island is one of the most remote places on Earth, and millennia ago, a crake landed on its shores. On predator-free islands energy-expensive flight is a hindrance to survival, so the crake's descendants gradually abandoned it. The Henderson rail has managed to avoid the fate of its flightless counterparts elsewhere. Quick on its feet and adept at hiding under vegetation, it has found strategies to avoid the Pacific rat, which now shares the island home upon which they are marooned forever.

▲ The Henderson rail is the sole surviving flightless bird in eastern Polynesia. Flightlessness made birds vulnerable to island invaders.

reach Pacific islands. The odds of any one species making a successful landing were tiny, yet a few succeeded. Later the Polynesians would face similar odds.

Island Ecology

Compared to mainlands, oceanic islands tend to have odd collections of species. Many families of plants and animals are absent, and ecological niches are sometimes left empty. Birds are often the dominant animals, since they can fly and reach islands relatively easily. Reptiles and insects are often common, but salt-intolerant amphibians and land mammals are usually rare. Before humans arrived in Hawaii, for example, there were no reptiles, amphibians, mosquitoes, ants or terrestrial mammals.

Nevertheless, islands can become evolutionary hot spots, filled with creatures that are endemic (found nowhere else). A single colonist may give rise to a spectacular diversity of new forms out of proportion to their mainland relatives. In Hawaii, over 55 species of Hawaiian honeycreeper sprang from one species of finch. The new forms exploited the island's empty niches, living in environments, eating foods or expressing behaviour not normally associated with that family of birds.

Island animals often evolve in strange ways, becoming giants, dwarfs, or losing the ability to fly. For instance, tiny islands in the Indonesian archipelago are home to the world's largest lizard, the Komodo dragon,

CROCODILE ON LAND

One of the most remarkable monsters the Polynesians met was the Fijian terrestrial crocodile (*Volia athollandersoni*). This 3-m (10-foot) crocodile had a short, dog-like muzzle and roamed Fiji's forests, preferring land to water. The formation of its bones suggests it behaved like Australia's Varanid lizards (goannas), digging burrows and climbing trees to hunt prey. Fiji, like many islands, is poorly studied and scientists suspect there are even stranger animals waiting to be discovered.

and miniature elephants and hippos once lived on a few islands in the Mediterranean.

Scientists are not sure why flightlessness, gigantism and dwarfism evolve on islands, but one explanation is the absence of large predators. A predator-free world also leads to tame behaviour and loss of defence strategies, making the animals particularly vulnerable if predators eventually invade.

FEATHER MONEY

In the Pacific red feathers were not just objects of beauty but a symbol of wealth and power too. They were traded for more expensive items such as canoes and brides, and taxes were sometimes even paid in feathers.

The association between feathers and status was especially strong in Hawaii, where chieftains and high-ranking individuals wore robes made of thousands of individual feathers. Feathers were also used to cover images of gods and to decorate crested battle helmets. Hawaiian bird-catchers trapped birds like the Mamo and O'o by smearing sticky plant resin on flowering trees and waiting for the birds to get stuck when they came to drink nectar. The most valued feathers were plucked and the birds were released alive. When enough feathers had been gathered, they were taken to a 'money maker' to be sown on to robes. Around 80,000 birds were needed to make a single full-length royal cape.

▲ These Hawaiian *Alu'ula* (sacred royal capes) each contain 450,000 feathers of great monetary value.

Feather money is still used in remote parts of the Solomon Islands. The red breast feathers of honeycreepers are sewn on to strips of material called *touau*.

Coral Gardens

When Polynesian mariners discovered an island, they faced many challenges. Throughout the Pacific volcanic islands are at different stages of erosion, so that each is unique and has its own set of problems. Far from being the idyllic paradises we imagine, many Pacific islands lack important resources. The first job of the newly arrived Polynesians would have been to assess what natural resources were available, and then attempt to adapt to that environment or leave. The sight of large native animals would have been celebrated, since they represented an important source of food.

Halfway between mainland Fiji and the kingdom of Tonga are the Lau Islands. This series of 60 tiny flecks of land is made up of coral atolls – rims of ancient, eroded volcanic craters that poke above the waves. Food and fresh water are sparse on these atolls, but beneath the waves are some of the world's richest coral reefs, teeming with fish and other seafoods. While these coral gardens provided the people of Lau with the basics, the lack of water and other resources meant they had to trade with larger islands to survive. They made craftsmanship their livelihood, trading carved hawksbill turtle artefacts and finely decorated tapa cloth for crops and other necessities. Their most famous products were mats of woven pandanus leaves edged with the red feathers of a parrot called the 'cooler bird'. This bird lived on the Fijian mainland, so to ensure a constant supply of feathers, it was trapped and caged, ready to be plucked as needed.

Easter Island

One of the most isolated locations on the planet is Easter Island, or Rapa Nui, which lies 3,200 km (2,000 miles) from the South American mainland and 2,300 km (1,400 miles) from Pitcairn Island, the nearest habitable land. Because of these vast distances, trading with other islands was impossible for the people of Rapa Nui. And unlike the Lau Islands, Easter

Island is not an ancient, weathered atoll with sheltered coral reefs, but a much younger island, its shoreline formed by steep cliffs that receive the full force of the waves. As a result, coral reefs are non-existent, so harvesting seafood was difficult and often dangerous.

On most Polynesian islands, kitchen middens – ancient rubbish heaps, studied by archaeologists – identify fish as the main source of food. In fact, 90 per cent of bones found in ancient Pacific refuse are from fish. But on Rapa Nui, less than a quarter of the bones discarded between AD 900 and 1300 were from fish. When it came to the sea, these islanders were big-game hunters, with porpoises making up a third of their protein intake.

Porpoises were the biggest animals available because there were no large land animals on Rapa Nui. However, rich seabird colonies provided an alternative source of protein – fulmars, albatrosses, boobies and frigate birds were all regular dishes, as were land birds like barn owls, herons and parrots. The islanders also raised chickens and caught Polynesian rats, which the founders probably brought with them deliberately. In fact, on Rapa Nui more rat bones than fish bones have been found in middens.

Rapa Nui may not have had large animals, but it did have an extra-ordinary megaflora. When the first islanders arrived, they discovered vast subtropical forests with unique daisy trees, rope-yielding hauhau and toromiro, with ferns and shrubs forming a dense understorey. Studies of ancient pollen deposits reveal that the most abundant tree was a monstrous palm. Now extinct, this palm was related to the Chilean oil palm, which grows to 25 m (82 feet) tall and 1.8 m (6 feet) in diameter. Like its Chilean relative, the Rapa Nui palm would have been a valuable source of edible nuts and syrup-like sap.

At first, Rapa Nui must have seemed like an inexhaustible paradise. The islanders made good use of its rich soils and became heavily dependent on the palm and their introduced crops of banana, taro, sweet potato

▶ These stone monoliths known as *moai* probably represented Polynesian gods and deified ancestors. Today they are icons of the island and the ecological disaster that occurred there.

and sugar cane. But their luck was not to last. Over time the forests dwindled as trees were cut for timber, firewood, or rollers to move the *moai* – the enigmatic stone statues that look out to sea. Without trees to protect the land, the thin soil washed away and crops began to fail. The clans turned on one another, battling for the scarce resources. Cannibalism flourished. Within 300 years a sophisticated culture that produced the only written language in Polynesia (Rongorongo) had collapsed in an environmental apocalypse, and its population, which had peaked at well over 7,000 people, plummeted to only 750. Today not a single native tree grows on Rapa Nui, and its only native land creatures are no bigger than an insect.

Hawaii

More remote even than Rapa Nui, the Hawaiian islands are 3,200 km (2,000 miles) from the nearest land, making them an oasis in the vast Pacific Ocean. When the first explorers set foot here some 1,200–1,600 years ago, they must have been amazed by the bounty of easy food they found. Teeming with life and isolated from the rest of the world for millennia, Hawaii had evolved a multitude of strange animals – insects had lost the power of flight; finches had become nectar-feeders; long-legged owls patrolled the beaches; and large flightless birds ran around the settlers' feet with no apparent fear.

The secret to Hawaii's riches lay in its recent geological formation. Hawaii is a chain of mountainous islands that stretch 2,600 km (1,600 miles) across the Pacific. They formed as the Pacific seafloor slid over a volcanic hot-spot, deep within the Earth's mantle, causing molten rock to build up until new islands had formed – a process that continues to this day. Most of the Hawaiian islands have existed longer than Easter Island, time enough for peaks and gorges to be carved out by the elements, creating many and varied habitats. Cascading waterfalls and streams feed luxuriant valleys with fertile volcanic soils, while around the coasts lie coral reefs and sheltered lagoons abundant in sea life.

FLIGHTLESS IN HAWAII

When the Polynesians landed in Hawaii they discovered an alien world. Many birds (and even flies) abandoned their wings, preferring to get around on foot. Ibises – tall wading birds noted for their elegant curved bills – became short-legged and lived on the forest floor. There they met giant crows that wandered in search of fruit and carrion, and rails that foraged like rats, gobbling up endemic snails and the eggs of other ground-dwelling birds. Even an unusual form of tropical earth-bound Canada goose stared at the new invaders as it plucked grass.

▲ Hawaii's flightless ibis abandoned the sky and waterside life to stalk the gloomy forests of the interior. Island isolation allowed birds to pioneer bizarre new lifestyles.

With this natural wealth, the Hawaiians fashioned a lifestyle based in equal measure on hunting, agriculture and fishing. So rich were the islands that Hawaii eventually became the most populated part of Polynesia. When Captain Cook discovered it in 1778, Hawaii had a population of 400,000–800,000 and a highly organized social structure, ruled by a noble class and royal chieftains. Everyone had their role in society, where cultivation and fishing were no longer family activities but civil engineering projects. The Hawaiians had moulded their environment with pioneering vigour.

Polynesians are expert gardeners, but the Hawaiians were the most successful. Organized work crews built massive earthen terraces on which the main crop, taro, was cultivated. Many other alien crops were grown, including banana, bamboo, breadfruit, wild ginger, yam, sugar cane, mountain apple, sweet potato and coconut. To water them, mountain streams were painstakingly redirected. Generations of Hawaiians drastically altered their island homes, clearing the lowland valleys of trees.

In sheltered lagoons they built huge stone fish-ponds. These had wooden grills facing the open ocean. Rising tides swept fish through the grills, and as the fish grew they became too big to escape, creating a ready supply of food. With their stone tools, humans had pioneered life in a new world.

Paradise Lost

Pacific islanders such as the Hawaiians were once considered the embodiment of the 'noble savage'. They inspired visions of people living in harmony with nature in a pristine Garden of Eden. The philosopher Rousseau pored over the accounts of Captain Cook in search of Utopia, and the artist Gauguin left his housemate Van Gogh to live among the noble people of Tahiti. Only now are we able to look objectively at the effect that the Polynesians had on the ecology of the Pacific.

Some scientists describe the human impact on Pacific ecosystems as one of the swiftest and most profound biological catastrophes in the

HAWAII'S GIANT DUCK

A bizarre flightless duck (*Thambetochen chauliodous*), measuring 1 m (3 feet) tall, once stomped through the forests of Hawaii on its stocky legs. *Thambetochen* means 'astonishing goose jaws'. This bird had horny 'teeth' protruding from its bill, which it used for eating ferns and other plants. Most ducks live in wetlands, but the Hawaiian giant duck led a forest life more like that of a wild pig. The females laid their giant eggs in hollows made in the ground.

Remains of giant ducks and geese have been found in kitchen middens. Did humans hunt these birds to extinction? Many missing Hawaiian bird species disappeared so recently that scientists can extract DNA from their remains. Comparison of DNA revealed that several extinct species of giant goose evolved from a single flock of Canada geese that was blown off course during a migration, colonizing Hawaii only 500,000 years ago. Nene geese are the only living ancestors of that flock.

history of Earth. In the last 400 years 80 per cent of documented animal extinctions happened on islands. And losses caused by prehistoric humans exceed even those of the last 400 years. With the exception of the Galápagos Islands, which remained undiscovered until 1535, probably no Pacific island now has an intact community of native species.

Hawaii has suffered the highest percentage of native extinctions of any landmass. Drs Helen James and Storrs Olson, avian palaeontologists at the Smithsonian Institution, believe that before contact with Europeans, 4 large flightless ducks, 2 or more flightless ibises, at least 7 flightless rails, 20 or so species of honeycreeper, and many more animals became extinct. Within an 800-year period a possible estimate of 51 per cent of the 98 native land birds were wiped out. After Europeans arrived 17 more vanished. Hawaii probably had around 1,029 native plant species when the Polynesians came, 90 per cent of which were found nowhere else on earth. Today, most land below 500 m (1,640 feet) elevation is dominated by exotic plants, and almost all native birds have abandoned these lowlands. What is left of Hawaii's wildlife remains under serious threat, and it is now known as the 'endangered species capital of the world'.

ALIENS AHOY!

The canoes of Polynesian pioneers were filled with alien invaders including plants, dogs, pigs, Pacific rats and even accidental voyagers such as geckos, skinks and snails and diseases like avian pox. Alien introductions had a devastating impact on island species: new predators ran riot competing for food and living space, or simply ate the innocent natives. Island animals are particularly vulnerable because their long isolation erodes their natural defences, making them tame, flightless or slow-moving.

▲ Pacific rats (*Rattus exulans*) were lethal predators to ground-dwelling birds and giant insects.

Even though it is predominantly vegetarian, the Pacific rat was one of the worst invaders, eating the eggs of ground-nesting land birds.

Madagascar

Madagascar is the fourth-largest island in the world and a little bigger than the state of California. It is big enough to think of as a mini-continent rather than an island. It formed around 88 million years ago after the vast supercontinent Gondwanaland was torn apart by tectonic forces. Madagascar was one of the fragments.

Cast adrift on this gigantic Noah's Ark was a range of prehistoric animals that now began to evolve in unique directions, spawning such weird descendants that some became the foundations for myths and legends. New forms of animals arose as Madagascar provided a safe, isolated haven for its castaways. Today the island lies only 400 km (250 miles) from the savannahs of Africa, yet it does not possess a single

▲ **Madagascar is a zoologist's dream as three quarters of its species are found nowhere else** **on Earth. Its geckos have become unusually important and evolved into many fantastic forms.**

cat, monkey, gazelle or zebra. Instead, other animals evolved to assume their roles.

As a result of its long isolation, Madagascar is a land of outstanding endemism, with many unusual species that are found nowhere else in the world, ranging from geckos that imitate lichen to agile lemurs. Seventy five per cent of its species are unique to the island. But before humans arrived some 2,000 years ago, Madagascar was even weirder. It was home to some of the most bizarre monsters the human race has ever encountered.

When the first Polynesian settlers reached Madagascar, they found gigantic birds tending nests containing a basketball-sized egg. As they explored the exotically weird forests of spiny trees and orchids, they came across strange insectivores, calf-sized primates, and an animal that seemed part-puma and part-otter. These animals must have been some of the most wonderful things humans have ever seen – a bit like walking through the pages of a storybook filled with imaginary monsters.

Monster Lemurs

Madagascar is known for its lemurs, a unique and diverse group of primates found nowhere else on Earth. Millions of years ago lemurs were found throughout the world, but they became extinct because of competition from more advanced primates. They may have colonized Madagascar after its separation from the large continents by hitching a ride on a raft of floating vegetation.

Before humans arrived, lemurs ranged in size from animals little bigger than mice to giants as big as gorillas. The 15 species of giant lemur were not just scaled-up versions of their cousins – they looked, lived and moved in unique ways. Some were terrestrial and walked on all fours like *Archaeolemur* and *Hadropithecus*. Others lived an upside-down life like sloths (*Paleopropithecus*), hanging from branches, and still others were ponderous vertical climbers like koalas, with long, dog-like snouts that may even have had short trunks (*Megaladapis edwardsi*).

The largest of the lemurs was *Archaeoindris fontoyonti*, which tipped the scales at a whopping 180 kg (400 lb), making it the size and weight of a silverback mountain gorilla. Since very few branches could have held such a colossal animal, it must have spent most of its time on the ground, browsing on low-level plants much as the extinct ground sloths of the Americas did.

There is some archaeological evidence to suggest that the early

GIANT FOSSA

Today Madagascar's largest native land predator is the unusual fossa. Measuring 70 cm (27½ inches) in length, it looks like a cross between several different animals. It has the build of a cat, a dog-like snout, teeth like a leopard's and whiskers like an otter's, and has webbed feet and retractable claws.

But Polynesian colonists encountered a much larger animal prowling the forests – the giant fossa (*Cryptoprocta spelea*). Built like a short-legged cougar, it was far larger and more powerful than its living ancestor. The living fossa provides us with clues about the lifestyle of its giant cousin. Today's fossas cruise the forest at night for sleeping animals. They are incredibly agile climbers, able to slip up and down trees with ease and leap between branches. Once they spot prey, they attack with lightning speed. Living fossas prey on Madagascar's lemurs, but the giant fossa went after larger game. Did they prey upon giant lemurs? Giant fossa remains have been found alongside these extinct lemurs. Archaeological

▲ A panther-sized mongoose greeted Polynesian explorers arriving in Madagascar. Did it prey upon people?

work in Madagascar has only just begun, and further evidence may come to light.

Fossas were once classed as felines, but Madagascar has no cats. Amazingly, they belong to the mongoose family. Fossas simply evolved to fill a similar ecological niche to cats, both in behaviour and anatomy – a process common on islands.

Polynesians both ate giant lemurs and used their bones and teeth for jewellery. Today Malagasy folklore refers to an animal called the *kidoky*, which palaontologist David Burney of Fordham University suggests was a large terrestrial lemur such as *Archaeolemur*. It apparently looked a little like a living lemur called a sifaka, but it had a haunting, whooping call like that of an indri. If disturbed, it ran away rather than escaping up a tree.

CONVERGENT EVOLUTION

Island animals, when isolated, sometimes evolve to look like and behave like unrelated animals elsewhere – a process known as convergent evolution. *Paleopropithecus maximus* was a human-sized lemur, weighing 45–90 kg (100–200 lb). It bore a striking resemblance to living South American sloths. *Paleopropithecus* was common in Madagascar's forests, with several different species. Its sloth-like adaptations include elongated forearms with long, curved digits. Scientists think this plant-eater lived only in trees, moving slowly upside-down or hanging from its hook-like hands and feet.

▼ Madagascar's sloth lemur evolved to look and move in an upside-down posture like South American sloths, an excellent example of convergent evolution.

The Legend of the Roc

Lemurs and fossas were not the only Madagascan animals that evolved into giants. The island was also home to the elephant bird – a relative of the emu that was nearly twice as tall as a man and possibly the largest bird ever to exist. This flightless giant seems to have survived until very recently. In 1658 Admiral Etienne Flacourt, the Governor in Port Dauphin in southern Madagascar, reported stories told by the Antandroy people about 'Vorompatra – a large bird which haunts the Ampatre [marshes] and lays eggs like the ostriches; so that the people of their places may not take it, it seeks the most lonely places'.

In medieval times Arab slave-traders who set up colonies on the northern coast of Madagascar also recounted tales of a giant bird, and their reports may have inspired the legend of the roc, or *rukh*. In *The Thousand and One Arabian Nights*, Sindbad the sailor is seized by the talons of a roc and carried away to a fabled island, where he sees the monstrous bird's eggs: 'After awhile my eager glances fell upon some great white thing afar off in the interior of the island and behold I saw a white dome rising high in the air of vast compass ... which I found to be 50 paces. I was certified that the dome which caught my sight was none other than a rukh's egg.'

The thirteenth-century Venetian explorer Marco Polo also heard stories about the elephant bird when passing through Arabia and China in 1294. He recounted them in a chapter on Madagascar and Zanzibar in his *Travels of Marco Polo*: 'The people of the island report that at a certain season of the year an extraordinary kind of bird that they call the *rukh* makes its appearance in the southern region. In form it is said to resemble an eagle but it is incomparably greater in size, being so large and strong as to seize an elephant in its talons.'

Marco Polo's story may be mixed up with tales of a real giant eagle that lived with pygmy elephants on the island of Cyprus. However, when visiting the Kublai Khan in China, Polo was shown the emperor's collection of *rukh* eggs and feathers – medieval curiosities brought from Madagascar by travellers.

EARTH'S BIGGEST BIRD

The elephant bird (*Aepyornis maximus*) was 3 m (10 feet) tall and weighed half a ton. It had enormous, chunky legs and, unusually for birds, three-toed feet that made its legs look like those of a dinosaur.

The Malagasy called the elephant bird 'Vorompatra', which means 'marsh bird'. Recent remains show that it lived in thinly forested marshes and wooded savannahs. It was a plant-eater, feeding on low vegetation or using its long neck to reach high branches, as giraffes do. During the breeding season, it is thought to have migrated from the marshes to coastal sand dunes, where remains of its basketball-sized eggs can still be found.

When the Polynesians arrived there were two forms of elephant bird – *Aepyornis* and *Mullerornis*, the latter less than half the height of the former. Both belonged to the ratites, a group that originated before the final break-up of Gondwanaland. Like living ratites such as ostriches, emus and kiwis, elephant birds had tiny wings and were flightless. However, unlike ostriches, which are fast and aggressive enough to defend themselves from African predators, elephant birds were stocky, slow creatures with apparently few predators.

▼ The elephant bird was probably the largest bird ever to have lived. It survived in Madagascar as late as the seventeenth century.

Elephant birds laid the biggest eggs known – one specimen was 90 cm (3 feet) in circumference and 30 cm (1 foot) long, with the capacity to hold 8 ostrich eggs, 1,800 chicken eggs or 12,000 hummingbird eggs. Indeed, it is physiologically impossible for an egg to be larger and still function. Elephant bird eggs were probably the largest single cells to have existed in the animal kingdom, being much larger than dinosaur eggs. The parents must have been blessed with great patience – it would have taken around 90 days for such huge eggs to develop and hatch.

The beaches where elephant birds nested are still littered with millions of eggshell shards that crunch underfoot, but bones of the animals are rare. Scientists think this is because the birds made seasonal migrations to coastal breeding colonies but spent the rest of the year inland. Fragments of eggshells, mixed with pottery or stained with charcoal, are sometimes found in ancient kitchen middens. It seems likely, therefore, that egg collecting played a more important role than hunting in the elephant bird's demise.

Going, Going, Gone

When the first settlers arrived in Madagascar, there were about 17 species of megafauna, all of which are now extinct. Today, there are no native land mammals or birds weighing more than 11 kg (24 lbs).

Radiocarbon dating suggests the megafaunal extinctions began 2,000 years ago, when humans arrived, and ended only about 100 years ago, when the Madagascan pygmy hippo was believed to have disappeared. Many animals, including all the giant lemurs, are thought to have perished only 500 years ago, when Europeans came to Madagascar. So were humans to blame for Madagascar's megafaunal extinctions?

Some scientists once thought climate change was the main cause; now few hold this view. In the last 3,000 years Madagascar has undergone several minor climatic fluctuations, but the fossil record suggests these had little effect on the animals. As vegetation zones shifted with the varying climate, the animals simply moved with them.

A few scientists think the megafauna may have fallen victim to a mysterious disease brought to the island by humans or the rats that came with them. With no inborn immunity to exotic diseases, island animals are especially vulnerable. The problem with this theory is that diseases tend to affect groups of related species, but the Madagascan extinctions happened across the whole animal kingdom – tortoises, pygmy hippos, primates, mongooses and birds all vanished.

The Human Factor

There is very little direct evidence linking the early Malagasy with the megafaunal extinctions. Only six or seven archaeological sites have been found that show a connection between humans and extinct animals, and from those only about a dozen bones display signs of being modified by humans. The oldest of the bones were marked by metal tools around 2,000 years ago.

However, while direct evidence is hard to find, circumstantial evidence suggests that the Polynesians had a devastating impact on Madagascar's wildlife. For one thing, most of the animals that died out were large, docile, ground-living and active by day – in other words, worth hunting and easy to catch. Significantly, most of the lemurs that survived are small and live in inaccessible forest canopies, and many are nocturnal.

But hunting may not have been the main cause. Today 90 per cent of Madagascar's indigenous plant communities have been replaced or degraded, and much of the damage probably occurred during the early settlement era. Some of the oldest archaeological sites reveal that Malagasy settlers introduced crops such as rice, bananas and cassava, as well as cattle, goats and pigs. Many of these settlers practised a form of agriculture called *tavy*, using fire to clear patches of forest for their crops and livestock. After harvesting crops, the farmers abandoned the impoverished soil and moved elsewhere, repeating the cycle and clearing yet more forest.

▲ Today, pygmy hippos live in West Africa. Madagascar once had two species. *Hippo madagascariensis* was smaller than modern pygmy hippos and may have lived solely on land.

Practised on a large scale, *tavy* can severely degrade tropical forests, but it seems that this was not the only cause of the extinctions. Scientists recently discovered a dramatic surge in the charcoal content of 2,000-year-old lake sediments in Madagascar – far more than would be expected from *tavy* alone. The charcoal deposits indicate a massive increase in forest fires. If the experts' interpretation is correct, the main culprits behind the early extinctions may have been nomadic pastoralists who deliberately torched vast areas of forest to flush out game and create pasture for their animals. As well as burning huge expanses of pristine habitat, these people put imported herbivores in direct competition with Madagascar's native plant-eaters – the elephant birds, giant tortoises, pygmy hippos and giant ground-living lemurs.

New Zealand

According to Maori folklore, Kupe – one of the great Polynesian navigators – left his homeland Hawaiki (probably in the Society, Austral or Cook Islands) and sailed south in search of new lands. While Robin Hood, the Crusaders and the marauding Genghis Khan were making history in the medieval Old World, Kupe discovered New Zealand. His wife named it *Aotearoa*, the 'land of the long white cloud'. It was the last habitable landmass on Earth to be occupied by humans.

The discovery was akin to setting foot on a new planet, for the Polynesians were not just the first humans but also the first land mammals to reach New Zealand. As if in a Hitchcockian fantasy come true, they had entered a world ruled by birds, and a kingdom overseen by giants. One was the tallest bird that ever lived; another was the deadliest aerial predator since the age of the dinosaurs.

Unlike Madagascar, New Zealand had never been colonized by land mammals – only flying animals could cross the violent southerly oceans that surrounded it. But like Madagascar, New Zealand was more of a minicontinent than an island, a fragment of the ancient supercontinent Gondwanaland. Being larger than the million Pacific islands put together, it must have seemed vast to the Polynesians. Perhaps they thought it was the mythical land of unending plenty they had dreamt about.

Bird World

During New Zealand's 80 million years of isolation, its birds had evolved to fill ecological niches normally occupied by mammals. Birds played the roles of big cats (the Haast eagle), forest elephants (moa) and even mice (Stephen Island wren). Thirty species evolved flightlessness. Others, like geese, coots, ravens and rails, grew to monstrous proportions, and most were fearless and slow-moving, since they had no ground-dwelling predators to evade. It must have been a surreal experience for the early settlers to meet so many animals that were curious rather than frightened of humans. The Polynesians would soon find that it was not the animals which walked on the ground that were to be feared – New Zealand was home to some spectacular birds of prey.

The fauna also included strange reptiles, primitive frogs that did not have a tadpole phase, and giant carnivorous snails that ate 30-cm (1-foot) earthworms. Many were relics from the long-lost world of Gondwanaland. This was also true of the plants. Around 80 per cent of the land was covered in primeval forests containing plants that would have been more familiar to dinosaurs.

HAAST EAGLE

The Haast eagle (*Harpagornis moorei*) was a terrifying killer of moa and other flightless birds. It was New Zealand's top predator until humans arrived, occupying the niche of a big cat. It had talons as big as a tiger's, and a 3-m (10-foot) wingspan, with females weighing 13 kg (29 lb). It was the largest and most powerful eagle ever to have lived.

Within New Zealand's forests, *Harpagornis* would sit high in the canopy and wait patiently for prey. Once it spied its quarry, it swooped down for the kill using its shortened, powerful wings to steer between trees. Its moa prey were often up to 20 times heavier, yet fossils show that the eagle killed them by driving its massive talons into victims' bodies, causing devastating internal bleeding.

The Maori etched pictures of *Harpagornis* in caves and carved its bones into tools. Some Maori legends refer to a mythical eagle,

▲ *Harpagornis* **may have looked like this. Did they prey upon the first New Zealand explorers?**

Te Pouakai or *Hokioi Hu*, that preyed on people. *Harpagornis* may have been attracted to Maori pioneers, who wore feathered cloaks and walked on two legs like moa.

The Moa

New Zealand's best-known giants were flightless birds called moa. Like elephant birds in Madagascar and ostriches in Africa, they were ratites — members of a group of flightless birds from Gondwanaland. The Polynesians were welcomed by 11 moa species in New Zealand, ranging from the turkey-sized *Pachyornis mappini* to towering *Dinornis giganteus*, which stood 3.7 m (12 feet) tall when reaching for food — twice human height. It was the tallest bird ever. All moa were flightless, and they were the only birds known to have been entirely wingless.

Moa were herbivores, browsing on shrubs and trees in New Zealand's vast forests, especially in the drier podocarp forests on the eastern side of South Island. Many of New Zealand's native plants have a fine lattice of tiny branches that evolved to protect their leaves from the beaks of hungry moa.

Each moa species had a distinctive build and beak shape suited to a particular lifestyle in the forest. *Euryapteryx* ate berries and succulent

◀ This mummified moa head was found in a New Zealand cave. Scientists at Oxford University have investigated cloning the moa from recovered DNA.

▲ This early reconstruction of *Dinornis giganteus* (with Maori medical students) is misleading. We now know that the moa only occasionally raised its head to full height as seen here.

◄ Some moa feathers have been found, enabling scientists to reconstruct their colour. It is thought that *D. giganteus* was similar in colour to spotted kiwis.

leaves, while *Pachyornis* fed on tough flax. *Dinornis giganteus* preferred the wide range of twiggy plants to be found on forest margins. We know what these birds ate because the contents of their gizzards have been preserved with their remains. Moa were alive so recently that often their feathers, skin and even DNA have survived, raising hopes that a living bird may one day be re-created.

Moa lived alone or in small family groups, occupying restricted home ranges that were probably fiercely guarded. Since they were scattered thinly through the forests, communication would have been important. Scientists believe they were very vocal, like the other antipodean ratites (the kiwi, emu and cassowary). The shape of the neck and throat of *Euryapteryx* suggests that the forests were filled with the sound of its booming, low-frequency call.

With so few land predators around, moa could afford to breed slowly; evidence seems to incate that they laid only one or two eggs at a time. A few fossil moa nests have been found, scooped out of the ground under rocky shelters.

Moa proved very useful to the Polynesians, who fashioned cloaks from their skin, carved ornaments and tools from the strong bones, and ate their flesh and eggs. They even used their eggs as water carriers.

Gondwana Lives

Though much of New Zealand's unique fauna has vanished, some very peculiar animals still cling on. Among them are the tuatara (*Sphenodon punctatus*) – a reptile now restricted to remote, rat-free islands – and the giant weta (*Deinacrida heteracantha*) – a mouse-sized cricket that is one of the world's heaviest insects.

When tuataras hunt wetas, they re-enact a prehistoric battle that was once witnessed by dinosaurs. The tuatara has changed little in the last 225 million years and is the last surviving member of an ancient order of reptiles that flourished in the age of the dinosaurs. A weird creature with a light-sensitive third eye on the top of its head, it hunts during the cool

▲ Tuataras are the sole survivors of an ancient order of reptiles that lived during the age of the dinosaurs. Far from mainland competitors, they managed to survive in isolation.

KIWI

Kiwis (*Apteryx*) are also relatives of the moa. Flightless and nocturnal, they behave much like hedgehogs, probing for insects, worms and larvae. Their nostrils are on the end of an unusually long and flexible beak, with which they can sniff out prey hidden in leaf litter or even underwater. Kiwis have the uncomfortable honour of laying the world's largest eggs relative to their body size – almost one third of a kiwi's body can be taken up by a single egg.

▲ Did kiwis escape extinction because they are shy nocturnal creatures?

DRAGON MYSTERY?

Maori legends refer to a fearsome, dragon-like reptile called *Kawekaweau*, which was brown with red stripes. It was said to hide under fallen trees and leap out at passing Maoris. *Kawekaweau* were long thought to be a myth, but recently a giant gecko specimen, 62 cm (24 inches) long, brown with red stripes and a mouthful of needle-sharp teeth, was discovered in the Marseilles Natural History Museum. Was this the *Kawekaweau*? Although not big enough to qualify as megafauna, it was huge compared to other geckos and it may have been one of New Zealand's most important ground-dwelling predators, feasting on small birds, giant insects and even nectar.

of the night and spends daylight hours asleep sharing the burrows of sea birds.

Wetas, known to Maoris as 'demons of the night', are also relics of Gondwanaland's ancient fauna. These huge, wingless insects can be bigger than mice and fill niches normally occupied by rodents. The giant weta is the largest species, reaching some 70 g (2½ oz) in weight.

The Vanishing

Now a deathly silence hangs over the forests of New Zealand, for its native fauna are all but lost. Few doubt that humans were responsible for this tragedy, and that climate played no role. The chronology of New Zealand's extinctions is a clear example of what can happen when humans arrive in an isolated world.

According to Maori folklore, a planned mass colonization began after Kupe returned to Hawaiki and announced his discovery of 'a distant land, cloud-capped, with plenty of moisture and sweet-smelling soil'. Today all of New Zealand's tribes, or *iwi*, are named after the canoes (*waka*) that their Polynesian ancestors are said to have come in. Evidence from archaeology and DNA studies suggests that no more than 200

Polynesians colonized New Zealand about 800 years ago, arriving in *waka* packed with livestock and tropical crops.

New Zealand presented the settlers with a major challenge. With a culture based on the constant warmth of the tropics, they now had to adapt to a temperate world governed by well-defined seasons; they were probably some of the first Polynesians to witness snow. Except for dogs (*kuri*) and Pacific rats (*kiore*), none of the settlers' livestock survived the colonization. Worse still, their tropical crops were ill suited to New Zealand's cold winters, and many failed to grow. The few that did survive (taro, yam, bottle gourd, paper mulberry and sweet potato) were confined to milder regions of North Island and the northern edge of South Island. When the first winter arrived, the settlers' prospects must have looked bleak. They probably resorted to eating the ground-up roots of forest ferns.

▲ The Maori brought tropical plants and animals from Hawaiki. Most did not survive the cold winters. The only animals to do so were dogs (*kuri*) and Pacific rats (*kiore*).

No More Moa

In South Island, where crops would not grow, the settlers quickly turned to big-game hunting. Large settlements sprang up at river mouths, where hunters had easy access to both the forests of the interior and the rich sea life. Fur seals were clubbed at their coastal colonies, while dusky and Hector's dolphins were harpooned from canoes. But the hunters had a particular taste for moa – they were easy prey and provided huge, nourishing eggs and enormous, succulent drumsticks.

In summer, when male moa were tending their eggs, armed hunters roamed the forests. Trackers searched for moa's food-trees, droppings and water holes, and set snares made of supple-jack vines. When they came across their quarry, they simply walked up the birds and clubbed or speared them to death. Heads and feet were cut off and discarded, and torsos were shipped downriver in reed canoes. Back at the settlement, moa were cooked in underground ovens (*hangi*) in huge meat-processing facilities. Skins were fashioned into clothing, and the strong bones were carved into ornaments, clubs, fish-hooks, adze handles and other tools.

Studies of midden sites reveal that moa provided 30–40 per cent of the islanders' calorie intake at the peak of the slaughter. Moa meat was so plentiful that much went to waste – often only the thighs were eaten and the rest was thrown away. Some of the meat-processing settlements grew to enormous sizes on their rich diet: a settlement at Wairau Bar measured 148 acres in size. In the nineteenth century train-loads of the discarded moa bones were mined from such sites and processed into fertilizer.

The glut of food caused South Island's population to surge to around 1,000, but the boom was not to last. Moa numbers began to tumble, and the hunters were driven to increasingly desperate measures. Charcoal remains reveal that fire was probably used as a hunting tool, with vast tracts of forest set alight to flush out the remaining birds. By the time the moa became extinct, around 40 per cent of South Island's forest had been destroyed.

The extermination of moa by the Maoris' ancestors was one of the world's swiftest megafaunal extinctions. For a long time scientists

▲ Maori women removing feathers from moa before cooking. At such special settlements, moa meat was cooked, skins were fashioned into clothing and their bones made into tools and ornaments.

◄ Moa eggs collected for food. Archaeological finds show that eggs were also used as water containers. Moa were gentle animals, making them vulnerable to egg collectors.

thought it took around 400 years for all 11 species of moa to die out. However, recent estimates, based on the moa's slow breeding rate, suggest it took only 50–160 years, though a handful of birds may have persisted in remote mountainous regions. Archaeological evidence supports these estimates: in a midden at Shag River Mouth, moa accounted for half the bones at the bottom of the heap but only 20 per cent at the top. The islanders used this midden for only 50 years.

A New Beginning

When the last moa finally disappeared in around AD 1400, hunger began to stalk the Maoris. The large meat-processing settlements disbanded, and people started living in smaller family groups. Not only were moa extinct in both North and South Island, but marine mammals were profoundly depleted, and Pacific rats had wiped out many of the ground-nesting flightless birds. So the Maoris began hunting New Zealand's smaller, flying birds. They were eating their way down the food chain.

But now there was a change in the islanders' attitude to the environment. The rapid demise of the moa, which had been abundant within living memory, must have been a shock; now they knew New Zealand was not an endless frontier, so they began to develop a new ethic, employing the traditional Polynesian system of prohibition and killing animals only at certain times of the year. Temporary reserves were set aside and guarded to protect animals while numbers recovered. Hunting the birds of the forest canopy became an art form. Bird *Tohunga* communicated with the gods and used their intimate knowledge of bird behaviour to trap particular species. Kaka parrots, for example, were

BATS THAT RAN

Before the Maoris, New Zealand's only native mammals were four species of bat, one of which – the greater short-tailed bat (*Mystacina robusta*) – recently became extinct. This unusual bat evolved the ability to scramble along the ground in a world free of other small land mammals. Pouches on the sides of its body allowed it to tuck away its folded wings, scurry down burrows, and dig through leaf litter like a shrew or rat. It drank nectar from flowers and was partially carnivorous, eating carrion and nestlings. Of New Zealand's two remaining bat species, the lesser short-tailed bat (*Mystacina tuberculata*) has a forest-floor lifestyle similar to its extinct cousin, while the long-tailed bat has a more typical bat lifestyle.

The Maoris called bats *pekapeka*, and associated them with death and destruction, although they were not averse to eating them. Bats were caught by smoking out their tree-hollow roosts until they became dopey.

195

caught using tame decoy birds. By pulling a string on the tame bird's foot or poking it with a stick, the hunter made the decoy screech and attract the attention of wild birds, which were then caught in snares.

On North Island the Maoris subsisted on a combination of hunting and agriculture. Using a slash-and-burn technique to clear the forests, they encouraged the growth of edible ferns and cultivated their main crop, the sweet potato. In contrast to the tropics, the New Zealand climate permitted only one harvest of the plant a year, so the islanders took to storing crops in thatched pits to tide them over the winter. In these pits they also placed smoked fish and birds preserved in their own fat.

Farmland expanded at the expense of forest, and bird numbers dropped still further. Tensions rose as rival clans began warring over their dwindling resources. By 1600 New Zealand was a land of starvation. But the final blow was yet to come – in December 1642 a Dutch sailor called Abel Janszoon Tasman sighted the coast of Westland; Europeans had discovered New Zealand.

Evidence indicates that most of New Zealand's animal extinctions happened before Europeans arrived. Thirty-five mainland bird species were exterminated after the Polynesian colonization and before the arrival

TIBBLES AND THE WREN

The Stephen Island wren (*Traversia lyalli*) was a tiny, semi-nocturnal flightless bird with a lifestyle similar to that of a mouse. Fossils show that it once lived throughout New Zealand, but was exterminated hundreds of years ago by the Pacific rat. By the time Europeans arrived, it was found on just one small island, in Marlborough Sound. The only European to see it alive was lighthouse keeper David Lyall, who arrived on the island in 1894. Lyall noted that the wren lived among rocks, darting about between them and hiding under them. This behaviour suggests that it was the only flightless perching bird ever to exist.

The last surviving wrens were eaten by the lighthouse keeper's cat, called Tibbles. Tibbles delivered 17 birds – the entire species – to its master as gifts. The Stephen Island wren probably died out within one year of the cat's arrival. It became extinct only a few days after being officially described – a world record.

of Europeans. What animals did survive were mostly confined to remote islands where humans and rats could not get at them. The arrival of Europeans was the final death knell for New Zealand's unique fauna. After British colonization 14 more bird species perished, making a total of 43 species – 51 per cent of native mainland birds.

The British brought more exotic species, including sheep, cattle, goats and horses. Rabbits began to take over the grasslands, so cats and stoats were introduced to get rid of them – but these new predators preferred

THE FANTAIL'S DANCE

Birds play a central role in Maori mythology and culture. Even today some Maoris believe that their souls take the form of birds.

The fantail is a restless bird known for its gesticulations. In Maori mythology it was also one of the warriors in a great battle between sea birds and land birds. When the fantail approached the enemy, he was in such a passionate rage that he jumped from side to side, glaring and performing all manner of movements. The *haka*, made famous by being performed before rugby matches, is said to be partly derived from the dance of the fantail.

▼ The *haka* plays a vital role in Maori culture. It is not only a war dance, but a ritual performed for many types of occasion, including rugby matches.

native prey. Marine mammals such as the fur seal were hunted with renewed vigour, and more forest was cleared to produce timber or open land for European crops.

End of an Era

The Polynesians had a devastating effect on the megafauna they encountered in New Zealand, Madagascar and the islands of the Pacific. Though later European colonists also had a dramatic impact, much was already lost by the time they arrived. This is not to suggest that the Polynesians were less environmentally friendly than the European settlers – far from it. Polynesian culture had a long tradition of environmental management, but they had the misfortune to discover the most fragile ecosystems on the planet: island species have difficulty surviving any new predators. Later they cleared the forests and became farmers; loss of habitat then became the driving force behind the extinctions. The arrival of Europeans was the final straw.

Today all that we have left of our planet's remarkable island fauna are tantalizing remnants. It is amazing to think how close we came to seeing the monsters of Madagascar, New Zealand, and the Pacific islands. Some endured while Arab slave-traders, pirates and explorers were discovering the world of the Polynesians. Moa walked on New Zealand, and the cries of giant lemurs still echoed through the forests of Madagascar while Shakespeare was writing his plays. One wonders what cruise-ship tourism would be like today had these creatures not died. When the Polynesians first arrived, they entered a strange world, and while they established themselves, they became dependent on hunting. The most vulnerable were the first to go – the tame, defenceless and flightless animals.

▶ Polynesian pioneers arrived in a land filled with a cacophany of bird-song. Today, the forests and their birds are gone. Now Maori and European conservationists are fighting to save what remains of the native fauna of New Zealand.

CONCLUSION

Compare two journeys: in August 2001 I paddled by kayak with my brother through a remote park in the vast forests of Quebec in Canada. In this seemingly endless wilderness we slept soundly in a tent without a rifle. In fact, in a journey covering 115 km (71 miles) we spotted only one species of megafauna – a black bear – and some moose tracks. Yet when I visited an African game park a few years earlier, I was instructed not to leave my vehicle because of the threat from animals, and at night I slept behind a giant steel fence tipped with razor wire. In one day in Africa I saw more species of large animal than a naturalist in the New World might see in a lifetime. Why does Africa have so many large megafauna and other continents so few?

We associate Africa with wildlife because it still has its monsters. In the past, the rest of the world was not so different, and the evidence is right beneath our feet. Buried in the ground below us are the remains of some of the most amazing creatures to have walked the Earth. They thrived for millions of years, evolving into monsters that we can barely imagine. But during the last stages of the Pleistocene epoch, they disappeared – victims of a mysterious extinction. The scale of the vanishing is startling: South America lost 80 per cent of its large animal genera, North America lost 73 per cent, Eurasia 30 per cent, Australia 86 per cent, and oceanic islands lost a staggering 95 per cent of their large birds and animals. So what happened to Earth's monsters?

Of course, all species eventually disappear. Over millions of years, new forms evolve and old ones fade away. However, the fossil record reveals several occasions in Earth's history when vast numbers of species died out *en masse*. Scientists traditionally recognize five such mass extinctions, the last of which wiped out the dinosaurs some 65 million years ago. Mass extinctions are normally identified by their impact on small marine creatures, whose shells fossilize well, but the end-Pleistocene extinction was different. It did not kill off enough species to qualify as a true mass extinction, yet it remains the most concentrated loss of large animals since the death of the dinosaurs.

Discovering its cause is important – the mysterious forces that destroyed the megafauna could perhaps threaten us. Many theories have been proposed to explain this event, but the best candidates are disease, climate change or human overkill. So which was the culprit?

Killer Plague?

A few scientists think that a highly infectious disease, perhaps transmitted by humans, was responsible. Two proponents of this theory are Ross MacPhee of the American Museum of Natural History and Preston Marx of Tulane University, Louisiana. As MacPhee and Marx point out, long-established diseases tend to evolve a benign relationship with their host so as not to destroy their own means of transmission. In contrast, newly emerged diseases, which can form when viruses or bacteria jump the species barrier, tend to be lethal. A good example is AIDS in humans, which began in the 1950s after the HIV virus jumped from African monkeys to humans owing to increased contact. Emerging diseases may be harmless to their ancient hosts but deadly to new ones, and they are more likely to appear when previously isolated species are brought together. Could increased contact between humans and the megafauna have triggered a lethal epidemic as prehistoric people spread around the globe?

One of the problems with the disease theory is that the megafaunal extinctions involved a broad range of animals, including mammals, birds and reptiles. It is unlikely that such diverse animals would all be susceptible to the same microbe. Even so, MacPhee and Marx have begun searching the tissue of frozen mammoths for bugs that could have caused a Pleistocene epidemic, but so far without success. Lacking concrete evidence to back it up, their theory remains conjecture.

Climate?

There is plenty of evidence that climate can kill. Each of the previous big five mass extinctions is associated with drastic global climate change. But what caused these temperature shifts, and was the same force responsible for the demise of the end-Pleistocene megafauna?

For most of the last century, scientists argued over why the dinosaurs died out, with nearly everyone agreeing that climate change was responsible. What they were really quarrelling about was what had caused that change. Sunspot activity, changes in Earth's orbit, continental drift, volcanoes and a cataclysmic asteroid impact were all proposed. The evidence was disputed for decades, until a giant impact crater was found in Mexico, the size and timing of which corresponded with a global layer of ash and iridium (an element rare on Earth but common in meteorites) in ancient rock strata. Did the megafauna suffer the same fate as the dinosaurs? Evidence suggests not. Scientists have found no big craters or iridium layers dating from the late Pleistocene, even though such evidence should be fresher and hence easier to find than that associated with the dinosaur extinction.

What about other causes of climate change? Continental drift cannot explain the end-Pleistocene event because there simply hasn't been enough time for the continents to move substantially. Similarly, there is no evidence of massive volcanoes or lethal changes in solar radiation.

In North America at least six mini-extinctions occurred in the last 10 million years, with the end-Pleistocene calamity ranking only second out of the six in terms of number of victims (though first in terms of its effect on large animals). The earlier extinctions all coincided with warming periods as ice ages ended, long before humans arrived. Some scientists think the driving force behind these extinctions was vegetation change, brought about either by dramatic swings in temperature or by an ecological ripple effect as key species vanished, disrupting ecosystems. Animals such as elephants can have a spectacular effect on landscapes, turning forests into grasslands and profoundly altering the fortunes of other species. Such habitat-change hypotheses are really climate theories at heart.

It is undeniable that climate change can destroy life. However, another strand of evidence reveals serious flaws in the climate theory — and points the finger of blame in a very different direction.

Human Arrival?

When Ice-age animals were first discovered in the nineteenth century, some palaeontologists proposed that hunting by humans was responsible for their disappearance. The most famous modern champion of this overkill hypothesis is Paul Martin of the University of Arizona, who argues that human hunters inadvertently exterminated the megafauna as they spread across previously uninhabited lands. There are certain facts about the end-Pleistocene extinctions that climate cannot explain:

1 The strange spread of extinction dates If global climate change killed off the megafauna, mass extinctions should have been roughly simultaneous. But North America's extinctions began about 12,000 years ago, Australia's were spread over a broader period centred on about 50,000 years ago, and the island extinctions began variously from about 4,000 years ago. These dates are far from simultaneous — but they do show a suspicious correspondence with the arrival of humans.

2 Size and lifestyle bias Climate and disease theories struggle to explain why large animals and flightless birds were most likely to perish, a pattern absent from previous mass extinctions. In Australia, Madagascar and the New World, survivors tended to be small, fast, poisonous, tree-dwelling or nocturnal, while the victims were often slow, ground-living and active by day. Climate change is unlikely to discriminate among these lifestyles; hunters would.

3 Bias towards naïve animals Many of the New World victims were native species without experience of modern humans. In contrast,

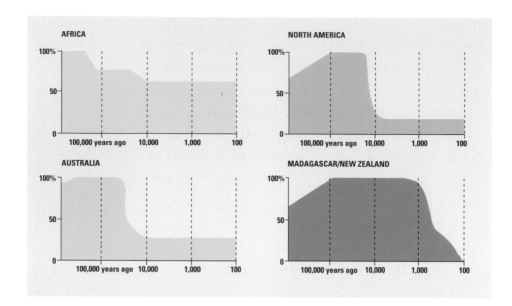

▲ Timelines for monster mass extinctions. Africa's megafauna coevolved with humans, perhaps explaining their survival. Extinction dates for other regions appear to coincide with humans' arrival. The graph for Eurasia (not shown) is similar to that for Africa, but starts later, with slightly more victims.

recent invaders from Eurasia (moose, elk, bison, caribou and muskoxen) survived. With little instinctive fear of humans, the indigenous animals would have been easy targets for hunters. Climate theories cannot explain why African and Eurasian megafauna fared better than their New World or Australasian counterparts, but the overkill theory can: animals that were accustomed to humans had evolved ways of defending themselves.

4 Delayed extinction on islands Megafauna thrived on islands long after the mainland extinctions. Woolly mammoths survived on Wrangel Island in the Arctic until 4,000 years ago, but disappeared from mainland America more than 10,000 years ago. Ground sloths survived in Cuba 4,000 years longer than in North America. The climate of such islands was not different from that of associated mainlands.

5 Reintroduced monsters thrive If climate-induced habitat change destroyed the megafauna, reintroduced relatives should have difficulty surviving in the new habitat. Yet horses reintroduced to the New

World by the Spanish have spread across the American West so successfully that they are now a pest. Similarly, European wild boar, llamas and capybara – all of which are related to extinct New World fauna – prosper in modern America, and muskoxen have been successfully reintroduced to their former ranges in Siberia, Scandinavia and Alaska.

A common criticism of the overkill theory is that there is little archaeological evidence to prove humans hunted extinct megafauna. But evidence does exist. In New Zealand vast piles of moa bones fill ancient Maori refuse dumps, while kitchen middens throughout Pacific islands contain the remains of numerous extinct species. In the New World mammoth bones bear telltale marks of butchery and weapon damage. In Eurasia there is evidence that our ancestors hunted aurochs and woolly mammoths. One site in Australia (Cuddie Springs) shows butchery marks on megafauna bones. Despite serious uncertainties over the dating of Australia's oldest fossils, it does seem puzzling that the continent's large animals and people appear to have coexisted for so long. Does this mean climate was to blame for the animals' eventual disappearance? Peter Murray of the Central Australian Museum thinks not. He suspects Australia's extinctions were caused not by hunting but by another form of human interference: burning. There is mounting evidence that the ancient peoples of both Australia and Madagascar used fire to change the landscape. Though Australia experiences frequent wildfires in the dry season, humans altered the natural cycle by setting fire to the continent at other times of year. Such a change would have had a profound impact on plant life, with inevitable consequences for animals.

It is tempting to try to make peace among the warring academic camps by arguing that Earth's monsters succumbed to a combination of factors – perhaps climatic change and human hunting combined to push giant animals over the edge? But while we struggle to unravel the full story, the weight of evidence so far points to one culprit: *Homo sapiens*. As our species spread throughout the world, armed with fire and weapons, we left a trail of death in our wake. Where once magnificent monsters roamed, there now stand vast swaths of silent forest – a world of boring uniformity, its giants annihilated. Had we become the monster?

Acknowledgements

Kathryn Holmes wrote Chapter 1, Amanda Kear wrote Chapters 2 and 3, and Annie Bates Chapter 5. Ken Tankersley proof-read Chapter 4 and the Introduction and provided moral support. Other scientists who contributed through conversations or by reading manuscripts include: Chris Stringer, Peter Murray, George Nash, Trevor Worthy, David Burney, Jack Cohen, Erik Trinkaus, Rod Wells, Dirk Megirian, David Bowman, Mere Roberts, Richard Holdaway and Storrs Olson. This work would have been impossible without their research and any errors are mine. Thanks to the indigenous peoples of Australia, Canada and New Zealand who shared their knowledge of their history; Sarah Lavelle, Shirley Patton, Nicky Copeland, Linda Blakemore, Ben Morgan and Martin Hendry of BBC Books; and Joanna Usherwood, Nasir Hamid and Sally Pocock for practical support and encouragement. Thanks also to the television team, Mike Gunton (executive producer), Charles Foley (executive producer for *Animal Planet*), Andy Byatt (series producer), Andrew Graham-Brown (producer), Bridget Jeffery (production coordinator) and Lea Aldridge (production manager). This project was inspired by conversations with Mike Gunton, Charles Foley, Phil Fairclough and Jared Diamond. I recommend reading Diamond's books together with those of Tim Flannery (below).

*Ted Oakes (*ted_oakes@hotmail.com)

Further Reading

Diamond, Jared. *Guns, Germs and Steel*, Jonathan Cape (1997)

Diamond, Jared. *The Rise and the Fall of the Third Chimpanzee*, Vintage (1991)

Flannery, Tim. *The Eternal Frontier*, Random House (2001)

Flannery, Tim. *The Future Eaters: An Ecological History of the Australian Lands and People*, Grove Press (2002)

Flood, Josephine. *The Archaeology of the Dreamtime*, 3rd ed., Angus & Robertson (1996)

Gamble, Clive. *The Palaeolithic Societies of Europe*, Cambridge University Press (1999)

Martin, Paul S. 'The Last Entire Earth', *Wild Earth* (1992), vol. 2. no. 4, pp. 29–32

Mithen, Steven. *The Prehistory of the Mind*, Thames & Hudson (1996)

Pielou, E. C. *After the Ice Age*, University of Chicago Press (1992)

Mulvaney, John and Kamminga, Johan. *The Prehistory of Australia*, Smithsonian Institute Press (1999)

Stringer, Chris and McKie, Robin. *African Exodus*, Pimlico (1996)

Tankersley, Kenneth. *In Search of Ice Age Americans*, Gibbs Smith (2002)

Wilson, Edward O. *The Diversity of Life*, Penguin (1992)

Index